THE AM

A ZIONIST ANALYSIS

by

BEN HALPERN

SCHOCKEN BOOKS • NEW YORK

To my FATHER
and
to the cherished
memory of
my MOTHER
who taught me
by example

First published by Schocken Books 1983
10 9 8 7 6 5 4 3 2 1   83 84 85 86
Copyright 1956 by the Theodor Herzl Foundation
Copyright © 1983 by Schocken Books Inc.

Library of Congress Cataloging in Publication Data
Halpern, Ben.
The American Jew.
Reprint. Originally published: New York: Theodor
Herzl Foundation, 1956. With new pref. and postscript.
Bibliography: p.
1. Jews—United States. 2. Zionism—United States.
3. United States—Ethnic relations. I. Title.
E184.J5H28 1983   305.8′924′073   82–16875

Manufactured in the United States of America
ISBN 0–8052–0742–2

Preface to the Schocken Edition

SINCE THE ORIGINAL publication of this essay, the world in which American Jews live has changed significantly. The generation for which the essay was written is passing into retirement, and new perspectives shape the vision of those who have followed. Yet, it is too early to reissue such a book, a tract for its time, as a mere matter of historical curiosity. A polemic so recently timely may be either wrong or right; it cannot protect itself from critics on the simple grounds of irrelevancy.

The original text has been reproduced without change. It not only provides a view of the American Jewish situation in the 1950s, applying and testing a Zionist analysis; it also serves as a forecast of the present situation and as a benchmark from which to measure it. Today it is both necessary and possible to check, and make explicit, the forecast implied originally. A "postscript" chapter has therefore been added, serving two purposes: it extends the discussion and makes explicit certain views which were challenged by critics; and it reconsiders some positions in the light of what happened in the 1960s and 1970s.

Like the original essay, the postscript summarizes discussions published earlier, on different occasions and in various journals or collective works. The notes, which indicate these sources, refer to more extensive discussion of the issues than the brief summaries here.

In my years as a teacher I have been lucky to find friends and students concerned with the matters that concerned me. Their critical and imaginative questioning of positions I took has been a constant stimulus to more precise and comprehensive formulations. I should like to record my gratitude particularly to Jerry (Jacob) Cohen, Hillel Levine, Ehud Luz, Paul Mendes-Flohr, Sharon and Jerry Muller, and, especially to Frances Malino and to Phyllis Albert, Ed Goldstein, and to my friend and editor, Bonny Fetterman.

Brookline, Massachusetts
October 1982

Preface

I⊤ IS A CONVENTION
observed mainly by academic authors to preface their works
with a statement acknowledging indebtedness for assistance
and assuming sole responsibility for the views expressed. If I
adopt this convention, it is not because I believe this essay has
qualities of an academic work, or am resigned to having it so
received. My reasons are other than these.

Readers familiar with current discussions of Jewish questions need not be told that the views here expressed represent
no attitude officially approved by any Zionist or other Jewish
organization. For those who may read this without prior ac-
quaintance with Jewish ideology, it may be necessary to stress
that the present analysis is an entirely individual statement.
The position taken would perhaps be shared in certain respects
by some American Jews, particularly, no doubt, among Zionists; but not only would such persons correspond to no existing
organized body—they would also amount to a very distinct minority in any American Jewish or Zionist organization. As for
the whole structure of the present argument, and all its details,
I do not imagine another person could be found who would
accept it without question.

This, then, is an individual expression, written because I
believe it states the factual situation of American Jews accurately, and published because the Theodor Herzl Foundation is
kind enough to believe that it can contribute to the collective
examination of problems which the Foundation has initiated.

The body of this essay and its notes indicate quite clearly
my indebtedness to the many writers who have given us careful
and penetrating analyses of the Jewish problem, not least

[ix

among them those with whom I have had to take issue. There are others to whom my overwhelming indebtedness is not, and perhaps could never be, expressed in specific references. But I cannot release this book without acknowledging my very deep gratitude to some friends who, more than any other, are responsible for the fact that it appeared: to Akiva Skidell, who first urged me to write it, and to Dr. Emanuel Neumann, whose kind interest made it possible for me to devote the last period of my work for the Jewish Agency to its preparation; to Moshe Kohn, for the tact with which he suggested very necessary revisions in my original draft, and to Pearl Silver, for the constant friendship and helpfulness she has shown me not only in this but in all the tasks we undertook together.

The essay is built upon numerous articles which appeared at various times in various journals. These have been cut up, reshuffled, altered, expanded and supplemented so freely that it might be difficult to disentangle the borrowings, but the following list indicates the major materials exploited: "In Defense of the American Chalutz," HECHALUTZ, February, 1937; "Reconstructionism," LABOR ZIONIST LETTER, July-August, 1937; "At Home in Exile," FURROWS, January, 1943; "On Assimilation: Neither Salvation nor Safety," JEWISH FRONTIER, April, 1945; "Letter to an Intellectual," JEWISH FRONTIER, December, 1946; "The Destinies of Negro and Jew," JEWISH FRONTIER, November, 1947; "Exile," JEWISH FRONTIER, April, 1954; "The Idea of a Spiritual Home," JEWISH FRONTIER, March, 1955; "A Jewish View of America," JEWISH FRONTIER, December, 1955; "America Is Different," MIDSTREAM, Autumn, 1955 and "Apologia contra Rabbines," MIDSTREAM, Spring, 1956.

New York
January 31, 1956

Contents

America
Is Different

THE TERCENTENARY CELEBRATIONS
of the American Jewish community, held in 1955, chanced
to come at a time when two conditions combined to heighten
our sense of a peculiar destiny. We American Jews, after the
destruction of the six million who were the main body of
Jewry and the immediate source of our traditions, remain
as the major part of all the Jews in the Diaspora. When we
think of this, as we cannot help thinking, we are filled both
with awe and with guilt at the blind whims of fortune
through which we escaped, and we are both oppressed and
uplifted by the leadership and new responsibilities we have
inherited.

There is another source, too, of our sense of a special
destiny. Since the Second World War, and especially since
Eisenhower's election, all America has been overwhelmed
with the feeling that now is our time of destiny, that this
century is the American Century. For it is either that or it is
the Russian Century, a thought that makes our distinction
not only a proud boast but a grim obligation. To be sure,
from the very beginnings of our history we Americans believed we were opening a new chapter, altering the whole
character of everything that had gone before. With Wilson
and F.D.R. we saw ourselves propelled into the center and
forefront of world events; yet we sometimes felt that these
great leaders were actually doing no more, though in the
distinctively American pragmatic fashion, than forcing us to
grow up to a point of social maturity the Old World had
attained before us. The end of the Second World War saw
the Old World in full collapse, while we (having elected
Eisenhower) looked back at what we had built, up to and

[11

under the New Deal, and sealed it as concluded, fully formed, a new American way of life worthy to be emulated by other peoples. In the period following the Eisenhower election, a mass of books, pamphlets and periodical articles appeared, all sounding in varying accents the same refrain: America is different!

The American Jewish Tercentenary celebrations came in upon the crest of this wave. Jews in America at their three hundred year mark have their own very strong reasons to underscore the theme that "America is different," and when they orchestrate this music, it is to a counterpoint of peculiarly Jewish *motifs*. America is different—because no Hitler calamity is going to happen here. America is different—because it has no long-established majority ethnic culture, but is still evolving a composite culture to which Jews, too, are privileged to make their characteristic contributions. America is different—it is not Exile, and whatever may be the case with other Jewries, the open doors of the State of Israel do not beckon to us. With such a rich choice of harmonies, is it any wonder that the Tercentenary celebrations of the American Jews swelled to a powerful chorus, elaborately enunciating the single theme, "America is different!"

It seems, however, that the crucial respect in which American *Jewry* is different was missed altogether in the Tercentenary celebrations. That is not surprising, because if this difference were stressed it could have made the whole occasion seem artificial and contrived. American Jewry *is* different from other Jewries. It is younger than any other significant Jewry—with the exception of the State of Israel. In terms of *real*, effective history we are far from being three hundred years old. There is good sense in Croce's contention that only the history of free, rational, creative effort is real history, and that the chronicle of events in which man is passive is a different kind of thing altogether. At any rate, if American Jewry has a truly distinct and individual character, giving it a destiny different from that of other Jewries, there is only one way it can have acquired it: only by freely, rationally, and creatively grappling with the specific problems of its existence, and then handing down its distinctive working hypotheses for elaboration by succeeding generations. American Jewry has had nothing like three hundred years of this sort of history. If there are any native American Jewish institutions that were initiated before the Eastern European immigration of the 1880's, then most of these, too, are creations of the middle nineteenth century. The earliest idea evolved and perpetuated to this day in American Jewry can be nothing younger than the Reform movement, which goes back in this country to 1824. The characteristic American Jewish type today is a second or third generation American.

We are, then, one of the youngest of Jewries, one of the youngest even of the surviving Jewries. Our real history begins *after* the "solution" in America of the most critical problem that faced other Jewries in modern times, the problem of the Emancipation of the Jews. This was the problem that other Jewries had to grapple with when they entered the modern world, and the various solutions that they freely, rationally, and creatively evolved for it gave them each their individual character. French Jewry dealt with the issues and problems of Emancipation differently from German Jewry, German Jewry differently from Austro-Hungarian or from Russian Jewry; but all of them had to deal with the problem, and there was a continuity and connection between the solutions they found. What is characteristic of American Jewry, and what makes us different from all of these together, is that we began our real history as a post-Emancipation Jewry. Emancipation was never an issue among us: we never argued the problems it presented in America, nor did we ever develop rival ideologies about it and build our institutions with reference to them.

Because of this, the continuity of European Jewish ideologies is broken in America. We never had ardent groups of partisans who saw in Emancipation the whole solution of the Jewish problem. In Europe the Zionist movement arose in opposition to this thesis, and proposed "Auto-emancipation" instead of "Emancipation" as the solution of the Jewish problem. The theory of "Diaspora nationalism"—the advocacy of minority rights as a solution of the Jewish problem—likewise opposed to the Emancipation principle of individual

[13

enfranchisement the view that the Jews must be granted autonomy as a group, as an ethnic entity. All these theories existed in America only as pale copies of the European originals.

We have in America a small group who vociferously defend Emancipation, the American Council for Judaism. The pointlessness of their propaganda is obvious to anyone who asks himself who among the American Jews is opposed to Emancipation. There is no such group or person, for no one proposes to undo what has been the accepted basis of our life here since before we made any effort to shape our American Jewish history. Nor does the American Council defend Emancipation as a *solution* for the Jewish problem. Their view would be more accurately expressed by a classic statement of Abraham Cahan's, who declared in 1890:

"We have no Jewish question in America. The only question we recognize is the question of how to prevent the emergence of 'Jewish questions' here."[1]

As for the opponents of this view, they, too, do not think in terms of a Jewish question which America has been vainly seeking to solve by the emancipation of the Jews, and for which we must seek alternative solutions other than Emancipation. We are only beginning to see what the Jewish question actually is in America.

Anti-Semitism and Assimilation

From a Jewish point of view, two elements are inseparable from any discussion of the Jewish problem: anti-Semitism and assimilation. For to a Jew the problem essentially is this: how can the Jewish people survive in the face of hostility which threatens to destroy us, and, on the other hand, in the face of a friendliness which threatens to dissolve our group ties and submerge us as a whole by absorbing us individually? Both phases of the Jewish problem are different in America than in Europe, and in both cases the reason is the same: in most countries of modern Europe the questions of anti-Semitism and the Emancipation and assimilation of the Jews were essentially connected with revolutionary crises in their national affairs, while no such connection existed in American history.

All we need do is consider what the Emancipation of the Negroes meant in American political and social history in order to measure the difference between a status that was never really contested, like that of the Jews, and one that it took a civil war to establish. Thus, when we think of anti-Semitism in such countries as France and Germany, Russia and Poland, we must remember that the great revolutions and revolutionary movements in those countries, at critical moments in their national history, placed the emancipation of the Jews upon their agenda for basic reform. Whatever has become part of the program of a national revolution not only divides the people at the first shock, but continues to divide them in the cycles of counter-revolution that always attend such upheavals in a nation's life. Hence, as Jewish Emancipation was an issue raised by the Revolution, so anti-Semitism had a natural place in the programs of European counter-revolutionary parties.

How different it was in America is quite clear. If the American Jews never had to divide ideologically over the issue of Emancipation, one of the reasons is that Emancipation of the Jews never became a revolutionary issue dividing the American people generally. For that matter, in the history of America the Revolution itself did not become a real (rather than academic) issue permanently dividing the people, since it was a revolution against outsiders—and the Loyalists remained in emigration. In England, on the other hand, the Cromwellian revolution was a crux in British history which still serves to determine opposed political attitudes. But at the time of that Glorious Rebellion there were practically no Jews in England. Consequently, at a later time, after the Jews had begun to arrive, the question of their Emancipation was debated in England (just as in America) in a relatively unimpassioned, desultory way. Whatever minor political struggles took place in spelling out the equal rights of the Jews had no inherent connection with, or essential place in, the major upheavals recorded in the national history. To be an anti-Semite in England, as in America, had no obvious, symbolic affinity with a counter-revolutionary

[15

ideology opposing the Glorious Rebellion or the American Revolution.

If one examines the American anti-Semitic movements, one cannot fail to appreciate how different they are from their European counterparts. Only in England do we find so anemic, so insignificant an anti-Semitic movement, a movement so unmistakably belonging to the "lunatic fringe."

The anti-Semitic movements of France and Germany, Poland and Russia may also have been fit subjects for psychopathological investigation; but no one will deny that they occupied a place in the forefront of the political affairs of their countries, and moved in (whether with or against) the mainstream of their national history. Far from being "fringe" phenomena, they had political power, or a reasonable chance to attain it. What we have in America in comparison is nothing but an aimless hate mongering. The kind of anti-Semitism common in America is, and always has been, endemic throughout the Diaspora. It may be found in every social condition and in every political persuasion, from extreme right to extreme left. It is an anti-Semitism of impulse: the most characteristic thing about it is that it is not really organized on the basis of a clearly enunciated program providing what ought to be done about the Jews if the anti-Semites had their way.[2] This is something quite different from an anti-Semitism that was primarily political in vision. Modern European anti-Semitism was characterized from the beginning by large and active political aims, and it included, among other far-reaching social revisions proposed in its counter-revolutionary program, precise provisions for making the Jews second class citizens, expelling them, or exterminating them. In comparison with these movements, American anti-Semitism (and, for the most part, British) has never reached the level of an historic, politically effective movement. It has remained, so to speak, a merely sociological or "cultural" phenomenon.

The question of assimilation also looks different in America, because the Jews never had an established status here other than that of our so-called Emancipation: there never were enough of us here before the nineteenth century to warrant giving us a special, institutionally established status. In Europe, on the other hand, Emancipation came as an effort to alter a hoary, time-honored status in which Jewish communities lived long before the Revolution.

The Emancipation seemed to promise the Jews that the difference between them and the Gentiles would be reduced to the private realm of religion. All public relations with the Gentiles would be carried on in the neutral area of citizenship, where Jews were guaranteed equality. Jews assumed that the public realm was identical with the whole social realm of intercourse between them and the Gentiles, and that in all other than purely Jewish, religious affairs they would have full and free contact and equal status with Christians. This they soon found to be a delusion, for in all countries they discovered that Jewishness was a barrier and a disability in a wide range of social relations and that citizenship opened far fewer doors than they had imagined.

In most European countries the areas closed to Jews had been elaborated by centuries of custom and usage. When one had explored the precise extent of new freedoms opened to the Jews by the new status of citizenship, the barred contacts remained clearly and decisively, in fact, often quite formally, defined. The army, the higher government service, the magistracy, and the universities were all careers closed to Jews which, by quite explicit understanding, became open immediately upon baptism.

In all of Europe, Jews soon found that even after Emancipation actual relations in society continued to be governed by a series of restrictions taken from the religiously grounded stratifications of the *ancien régime*. To protests that all this was contrary to the new doctrine of citizenship, purporting to open all careers to talent and all doors of social intercourse to individual merit, an answer was soon provided: a still newer doctrine, the doctrine of romantic, organic nationalism, superseded the principle of citizenship. The national idea gave a new justification and pumped new life into practices which had theretofore survived as stubborn relics of feudalism and now all at once became grafted onto the modern idea of democracy. Fixed social positions, traditional folkways and culture, inheritance of privileges and obligations—all that had once been grounded in the divine will—now gained an organic sanction in the national history. The Jews found their assimilation even more rigidly opposed than under the purely religious criterion. If inheritance (that is, ethnic origin) became the key to admission into society and the license for participation in culture, then even the formal step of conversion was of no avail to the Jew.

In the beginning of the present century the actual social conditions that faced the Jew seeking to be part of his European nationality represented a shifting balance between divergent tendencies. One tendency was that of the Revolution, whose principle was to treat the Jew as an individual no different from all the rest. Actual social relations conformed to this principle only to the extent that the Revolution itself, or other forces, had succeeded in atomizing society. The Industrial Revolution and the development of trade allowed Jews to find new opportunities in business and thereby brought them into a new relation of equality with Gentiles. The Revolution succeeded in imposing its own principles in all political relationships except the bureaucracy. But the Jews could not simply move into these new positions unaltered. The grant of equality imposed its conditions and demanded its price. The "clannish" solidarity of the Jews had to be given up so that they could enter the body of citizens as individuals. They could keep their religion as a private cult, but not necessarily the kind of religion that was traditional among them. Jewish tradition was too organic in its own way, it incorporated too much historic distinctiveness and ethnic character, for the rigid individualism of radical revolutionary doctrine. Not that anyone expected to see the full consequences of egalitarian theory rigorously applied to Gentile society. But the revolutionary ardor to liberate the Jews had roots of its own in the anti-Semitism that is endemic in all Gentile society and expresses itself in all its divisions. The Jews might not get all they expected out of Emancipation, but the Emancipators were disposed to watch with a jealous eye how the Jews went about paying its price.[3]

The nobility, the army, the universities, all the corporate embodiments of privilege bearing upon them the stamp of consecration and tradition escaped the levelling influence of Revolution. As Jews rose in society through other channels they found their ultimate elevation blocked at these points Some fought their way through to these positions as Jews, but most found that access to their goal, otherwise blocked, became magically open through a relatively simple and quite perfunctory (in most cases) operation. So they acquired new "convictions" and became baptized.[4] To the other Jews, this renegadism, as they regarded it, was their first great shocking disillusionment with the Emancipation, the first disclosure of the human degradation which is the price of assimilation.

The most serious strain upon Jewish-Gentile relations was the rise of counter-revolutionary anti-Semitism, which absorbed into an ethnic pattern the basic attitudes to the Jews implied in their old feudal, religiously determined status. Conservative anti-Semitism in an officially liberal society had contented itself with excluding Jews from those areas of corporate traditionalism which the Revolution had not succeeded in atomizing. But now nationalistic counter-revolution, seeking to turn the clock back, opposed the penetration Jews had already made into areas opened up by liberalism. Economic boycotts of the Jews were resorted to in order to bring industry and commerce "back" into the hands of the Germans or the Poles, or whatever the ethnic majority might be.

Particularly did the nationalists resent the great participation of Jews in all cultural activities. The organic doctrine of nationalism sought to overcome a cleavage between culture and tradition that had existed in Europe since the Renaissance. Modern culture had become a secular realm parallel to the traditional beliefs, art forms, ceremonials and etiquette still grounded in religion. The social framework of culture, the *Gelehrtenrepublik,* as the eighteenth-century Germans called it, was a liberal, international, individualistic, and secular intercourse between free spirits, which, even before the Revolution, existed side by side with the corporate social structures where the religious, feudal tradition was fostered. The Revolution was the signal that gave the Jews entree into this world. It was a liberty that they eagerly embraced, shut out as they were on other sides from assimilation and its rewards. But it was a main object of counter-revolutionary nationalism to bring all culture back into an organic coherence based on the national tradition, even if both the religious and the secular were adulterated as a result. This meant imposing upon all forms of creative expression the same corporate principles and ethnic criteria that regulated participation in the religiously grounded forms. The participation of Jews in any cultural form was henceforth regarded as an illegitimate intrusion, or even a plot by the enemies of the people to corrupt its national spirit.

Thus there were forces in European society determinedly striving to undo even the amount of assimilation Jews had achieved. They were opposed not only to the integration of the Jew into such social relations as were governed by liberal principles but also to the admission of the Jewish convert into social relations still governed by corporate, religiously grounded criteria.

How different was the situation here in America! Here the bare conditions of geography and social statistics made liberalism the dominant principle of social organization. It was not so much revolution against an old regime that opened the door to assimilation for the Jews; it was the large extent of sheer formlessness in American society which allowed Jews and many other heterogeneous groups to live side by side, with the forms of their readjustment to each other to be determined.

Free entry into American society, of course, had its price and also its restrictions, just as did the assimilation of the European Jews after Emancipation. The price of the freedom to let the ultimate forms of mutual relationship between immigrant Jews (like all immigrants) and the whole American community remain for the future to determine was the willingness of the immigrant to give up old inherited forms. Just as settled America was willing, within limits, to be elastic, so it demanded of immigrants wishing to be naturalized that they first of all be elastic and accommodating. Not that there was any haste about the scrapping of outworn Old World customs. America was large enough to set aside "ghettoes" in its cities or even whole regions in its broad lands where immigrants could live undisturbed more or less as they had been accustomed to live in the Old Country. But this was a provisional form of living, in effect outside the real America, which everyone expected to be superseded as the forms of true American living were worked out by immigrant and native Americans in a continuing process of give and take.

The willingness to relinquish Old World habits was the *price* of assimilation in America. Its *limits* were defined by the established prerogatives of the older settlers. It is true that the ultimate forms of American life remained—as they still remain—in principle undetermined, and our assumption is that the cultural contributions of all America's components are equally welcome. Yet it is both implicitly and explicitly assumed that those who came here first are entitled to preserve and impose such forms of living as they have already made part of the American way. America is not only in essence free and democratic; it is also, in its established pattern, Anglo-Saxon, religiously multi-denominational, and dominated by the mentality of white, Protestant, middle class, native Americans. However, this social dominance and cultural predominance are maintained not by delimiting any areas of social life under traditional, religiously grounded, and formally elaborated codes of exclusion which reserve them for particular families or religions, as in Europe. Our American history has not been long enough for that, perhaps, and in any case it has from the start consecrated the principles of complete social mobility, denying in theory all exclusions. But the claims and privileges of the older settlers are maintained by informal, almost tacit social covenants, which only rarely (as in our Immigration Act) need to be openly voiced.

Thus if liberal principles fail to be actually observed in America, just as in Europe, and if assimilation stops short at the barriers set up to protect inherited privilege, there is at least this difference: in Europe, the status with which we begin is the historical, quasi-feudal status, and liberalism

[21

rules only those areas which it specifically conquers; in America, the initial status is that of freedom, and only experience proves what areas privilege has successfully reserved for itself. Those in America who nurse a nostalgia for historically rooted social status have not been able to swim in the midcurrent of an American counter-revolutionary movement. The American Revolution is the very beginning of our real history, and there is no one who more proudly flaunts it as his symbol than the American conservative. The self-conscious American opponent of the liberal revolution has no real alternative but to become an expatriate.

The result has been that while the history of American Jewish assimilation, too, has been full of disappointment and unanticipated checks, it has run a characteristically different course from the European experience. At the very outset of the European Emancipation, Jews were brusquely confronted with the price they must pay: for freedom of the individual, virtual dissolution of the group. The immigrant to these shores, too, found that the prize of Americanization was to be won at a price: by unreserved elasticity in discarding everything which America might find foreign. In both cases, only religion was reserved as a sanctuary of Jewish tradition. But there were these differences: in Europe, there was a fixed pattern that Jews were expected to adopt in discarding their own customs; in America, the ultimate American way of life was still in principle to be determined, taking into account what of their own immigrants might succeed in "selling" to the whole public. Besides, the demands of the European Emancipation upon the Jews were peremptory, they had to be conceded at once, and even through a formal declaration such as Napoleon extracted from the French Jews. In America, there was no urgency about the procedure. The Jews, like other immigrants, could make their way into the real American community as swiftly or as slowly as they themselves chose. They could, if they preferred, remain in their ghetto seclusion indefinitely.

In Europe, then, the stick; in America, the carrot. A parallel difference existed when the Jews came up against the unexpected barriers to assimilation, the reserved areas not governed by liberal principles. In Europe, the principle of exclusion was clear-cut, traditional—and quite simply overcome, if you wished, by conversion. There was no such clear choice in America. Established privileges were no less alien to this country than an established church. It was neither the accepted practice to demand conversion for specific social promotions, nor to grant them upon conversion. Thus, if American Jews went over to Christianity, it was no such concerted wave as arose in Germany, in the first eagerness to overleap the unexpected sectarian barrier to full assimilation. It was rather a final seal, in individual cases, upon assimilation otherwise complete.

The Patterns of Modern Jewish Thought

It is clear, then, that the typical situation faced by the American Jew was not the same as that characteristic of the European Continent. The differences apply to both major aspects of the Jewish problem, to anti-Semitism and to assimilation. But modern Zionism, and indeed all modern Jewish ideologies, arose when Jews began to confront, to take account of, and to understand—or try to "reach an understanding" with—the typical situation of Continental Europe. The characteristic American Jewish situation had hardly even begun to be faced—until the establishment of the Jewish State abruptly forced us to face it. It need not be surprising, then, if at precisely this time we witness a feverish effort to create a new American Zionism and new American Jewish ideologies generally; nor that these forced-draught efforts should in the beginning often bring more confusion than enlightenment.

What was the historical situation of Continental Jewry in the late nineteenth century, when the modern Jewish ideologies arose? As we have seen, it was characteristically a period of post-revolutionary or, if we may say so, neo-traditionalist nationalism, a period with a living memory of an *ancien régime,* a revolutionary movement, and a wave of post- or even counter-revolutionary reactions. Moreover, the Jewish problem was intimately involved with every phase of that living tradition.

The spirit of that time was critical of the Enlightenment and the Revolution, of rationalism, capitalism, and social relationships based on the undifferentiated equality of citizenship. For the modern European, the Jew became a symbolic embodiment of all these discredited traits. The out-and-out anti-Semites (but not only they) regarded the Jew as the head and fount of everything they despised in the liberal revolution—its rationalism, capitalism, and principle of civic equality. Similarly, of course, the eighteenth-century rebels against the *ancien régime* had seen in the ghetto a symbol of the medievalism they were determined to uproot. And just as the Revolution had proposed the assimilation of the Jews in all respects except as a reformed religious sect, so, by a reversal of history, the critics of the Revolution wanted to solve their Jewish problem by halting or annulling the assimilation that had already taken place and eliminating Jews and Jewish influence from the new order they hoped to set up.

What made one a modern Jew in the late eighteenth century was to understand and accept the attitude of Gentile contemporaries to social problems, and to the Jewish problem among them. The modern Jews of that time accepted the demands of the Enlightenment to change their habits and customs—those relics of medievalism—in order to enter a new enfranchised status; on the other hand, they could not understand or accept the exclusions still practiced against them after they had paid this entry fee. But the modern Jew of the late nineteenth century "understood" fundamentally, however much it may have pained him, why it was that he was not assimilated into full fellowship in his country. He shared with the modern Gentile the feeling that European society had not yet become what it should be, or that it had even gone quite astray from its true path. Thus, integration into society on the basis of the liberal principles of the Revolution no longer seemed to be the solution of his Jewish problem. In fact, the degree to which that integration had already taken place, in culture, in economic pursuits, and even in political participation, began to constitute for him, as for the Gentile, the very crux of the Jewish problem, the false position in which both danger and self-denial dwelt.

He, like the Gentile, began to see or foresee other solutions of the Jewish problem as part of a new revolution of the whole structure of European society, in the course of which Jews would either disappear entirely as an entity or regroup in a new segregation from the Gentiles. "Modern" Jews hoped either for a radical revision of the liberal revolution, leading to Socialism and the disappearance of Judaism together with all other religions, or for a new nationalist era in which Jews would live as a distinct national entity, in the places where they then lived or in a new national territory. In other words, either total assimilation in a new, millennial secular society, without the eighteenth-century reservation of freedom to maintain a reformed Jewish religious community, or the total rejection of assimilation and an attempt to establish a new Jewish ethnic independence, in the several countries of Europe or in a new territory to be colonized by Jews.

The rejection of assimilation was a doctrine shared by Zionists with other ethnic autonomists. The failure of Emancipation, from this point of view, demonstrated that there had been a breach of faith by the Gentile Emancipators and a historical error on the part of the Jews; for after the latter had practically reformed themselves out of existence as a historic group, Gentile society had failed to keep its part of the bargain by assimilating the Jews individually. Zionism, however, viewed not only eighteenth-century Gentile liberalism with a disenchanted eye. It also had its reservations concerning those Gentile movements which, like itself, were critical of existing society and hoped to reconstruct it. In this respect, Zionism differed sharply from other modern Jewish movements. Jewish Marxism, regarding the Jewish problem as an expression of capitalism that would disappear in the classless society, implied faith that one's Gentile fellow-Socialists would not break their covenant as had the Gentile liberals. The advocates of national autonomy for minorities in Europe similarly trusted that Gentiles would abide by the covenants that were to embody this principle. Zionism had no faith in the willingness of the Gentiles to extend a welcome to Jews, under any definition, as free and equal brethren in the same land. It was a disillusionment built upon the experience that it was possible for revolutionists to regard Jewish blood spilt in pogroms as merely "grease on the wheels of the revolution."[5]

Zionism took anti-Semitism seriously and expected it to persist. This is the specific way in which it differed from other modern Jewish ideologies. The Socialists, who expected to submerge the Jews in a classless, cosmopolitan society, the Diaspora nationalists, who planned for minority rights—none could hope to succeed unless anti-Semitism vanished. The Zionist (and territorialist) solution of the Jewish problem, contemplating the removal of the Jews from Europe, remained intrinsically possible even if one were pessimistic or prudent enough to reckon with the persistence of anti-Semitism among the Gentiles.

Zionism, like other modern Jewish ideologies, felt it understood the critics of European liberalism (among them, the anti-Semites) and their disapproval of the liberal solution of the Jewish problem. Accepting, as they did, the organic, ethnic views of history and nationality, they felt it was a betrayal both of the Gentile and the Jewish national destiny for Jews to make themselves the protagonists of Gentile culture, for example, instead of fostering their own. Moreover, they appreciated that if it were the aim of a group to use all sources of power in a given territory for the preservation and propagation of its distinct national values, its traditional style of life and culture, its own ethnic variant of Christian culture, then it was bound to be resented when political and economic power came into the hands of Jews. Such an attitude left only one possibility for a compact between Jews and Gentiles that the two distinct groups could loyally uphold: those Jews who could not or would not assimilate must have a country of their own where they would be separate and independent.

Two things are characteristic of American Jewish ideologies. The first is that American Jews never faced directly the whole historic complex of problems, centering around Emancipation as a traumatic event, from which modern Jewish ideologies arose. The second is that only in our own time, actually in these very years since World War II, has American Jewry been compelled to face its own peculiar situation and to create its own history. One could conclude, then, that American Jewish ideological development may still not really have begun.

Whatever truth there may be in such a conclusion, it need not mean that we have had no differences of opinion, no debates until now. That is obviously untrue, for whatever ideology existed in Europe has had its adherents, few or many, here. Thus American Zionism, for example, arose by understanding and sharing in the typical attitudes, problems, and situation of Zionism in Europe—especially in the degree that American Zionists continued in America to live the life of the Old Country.

Now it was quite generally characteristic not only of American Zionism, or of American Jewry, or even of all immigrants, but of America itself to share and understand the life and thoughts, the trends of modern culture and politics in the Old World. Those newcomers who lived in the immigrant ghettos (at least, the cultural elite among them) shared the life of the Old World most directly and most specifically. Those older settlers (again, the cultural elite among them) who were establishing the permanent forms of American life also continued to live in the current of European political and cultural development, though with greater detachment and in a more general form. It was a more international European culture, and not so specifically a particular national culture, in which they shared. As for the culture arising in America itself, the specific "culture" native to the immigrant ghettos was based not only on an obviously transitory experience but also on an experience of suffering rather than of creation; "permanent" American culture remained intrinsically open and partially unformed, constituting, in a way, a set of defensible hypotheses rather than a body of axioms and absolute values.

It is important to note that only in our own time has the characteristic American Jewish type come to be the native-born American Jew. American Zionism, product of an earlier generation, was to a large extent a movement of the

[27

American immigrant ghetto.[6] Thus, intellectually, it shared in and understood the Zionism of the nineteenth-century "modern" European Jew, just as the other immigrant ghettos shared in and understood the social and intellectual movements of the Old Country they came from. The immigrant intellectuals who dominated American Zionism had a more direct and more specific understanding of the situation, problems and attitudes of the modern European Jew than is possible for the native American Jew. Yet even for them European Zionism was a *vicarious* experience.

It was natural, therefore, that even for the immigrants, new American experiences—the experience of the American immigrant ghetto, and the unfolding experience of the New American Society in formation—began to color their Zionism. This tendency was heightened by the influence of native American leaders who were active in American Zionism from the very beginning. The nuances by which American Zionism was touched through its naturalization in America have now, in a time when American Jewry is largely native-born and remains as the major surviving Diaspora, become the dominant coloration of a new American Zionism.

The two major divisions of the Jewish problem, assimilation and anti-Semitism, look different against an American environment. The theory of assimilation as a solution of the Jewish problem was a revolt against an old-established historic status of the Jews in Europe, into which they had sunk vast creative energies. The "Ghetto" in Europe was not only an oppression the Jews suffered but a way of life they clung to. And when the reaction against assimilationism came in European Jewry, it paralleled, in a way, the post-revolutionary movements among the Gentiles: it saw itself as the synthetic conclusion of a Hegelian dialectical process. The Emancipation had been an antithesis of an original thesis, the Ghetto; and Zionism (like other modern Jewish movements), in transcending the Emancipation, intended to absorb what was valuable not only in the liberal revolution but in the primary status—the Ghetto—which assimilationism had rejected.

"Assimilationism" in America was a rejection of life in the immigrant ghetto. But life in the tenements had never been filled with any creative significance, no historic values had been placed upon it and institutionalized through it, it contained no unfulfilled promises, no high demands spontaneously arising from its own context to give historic dimensions to its past and historic perspectives to its future. The immigrant ghetto from the beginning was entered into only to be abandoned. For the Jewish immigrants it represented either the collapse and bereavement of the old values of the true, historic, European Ghetto—or, if they had already emancipated themselves from the historic Jewish values, it was a "melting pot," a grimy anteroom to the real America, a sordid extension of Ellis Island.

The generation that entered the immigrant ghetto was confronted by one overwhelming task: to get out, or enable the next generation to get out. This task they accomplished. But the generation that accomplished it had, in a way, stepped out of the frame of history, for history consists in whatever continues over a span of successive generations. The immigrant ghetto was not a continuation of the context of European Jewish life, whether Ghetto or emancipated; it was an interruption of that continuity, a break with that context. Nor did it, nor was it ever intended to, continue into the life of the next generation. It was a specific experience outside the frame of history and hence outside the frame of culture, at least in so far as culture is essentially historic.

There was nonetheless a very active cultural life and a vivid sense of history in the Jewish immigrant ghetto. That generation, in fact, reached an unsurpassed peak of historical awareness as Jews. And, concomitantly, they led a life of high cultural intensity. But the historical movements and cultural trends in which American Jews participated were European Jewish history and European Jewish culture, relevant to the situations and problems and expressing the values of European Jewry. The social reality of American Jewry was the one-generation experience of the immigrant ghetto, known from its very inception to be out of the frame of history and culture. Of course, American Jewry could never accept a merely vicarious participation in history and a merely nostalgic participation in culture, however intense these might be. The immigrant generation felt itself to be as much (if not more) a new beginning as a final chapter in the historic and cultural continuity of the Jews. They looked to the day when the threads of vicarious history and cultural nostalgia would weave into a new American pattern of continuity. But every American Jew, whatever his ideological sympathy—religious or secular, Zionist or non-Zionist, "survivalist" or "assimilationist"—knew beyond any question that the new hoped-for continuity that would transmit the American Jewish experience into history and culture must necessarily begin beyond the threshold of the immigrant ghetto.

If, then, "assimilationism" means radically to reject the "institutions" of the ghetto—in America, of the *immigrant* ghetto—then every American Jew, whatever his ideology, is an "assimilationist." And, in fact, the actual process of "assimilation" in the United States *is* the absorption of immigrants out of the immigrant ghettos. This is a movement in social relationships which it is common ground for every American Jew to accept. When "assimilation" served as an issue between American Jews it was not the actual process of assimilation out of the immigrant ghetto into the real American society about which they were debating; their argument was about assimilation as it occurred in Europe.

The differences of opinion native to the American Jewish experience are only now beginning to be defined. They arise after assimilation out of the immigrant ghetto has not only been tacitly accepted in principle but carried out in practice. Assimilation can only become an issue, in terms of the actual experience dividing the American Jews, after the liquidation of the immigrant ghetto. At that point, when he is an "integrated" member of American society, the American Jew—now typically native-born—discovers that he still has a problem of assimilation. The problem is a totally new one, it presents the first challenge whose creative mastery might establish a continuous American Jewish historic tradition. If we may speak in terms of the Hegelian dialectic at all in America, then we are only at the point of establishing a thesis, not, as in Europe, capping an historic antithesis with its synthetic resolution.

In view of this fact it should not be surprising if American Jews are unwilling to begin their history with the disillusioned conclusion that they can come to no satisfactory terms with the Gentiles for the creative survival of the Jewish people in America. Nor should it be surprising that in looking backwards for its supports in history, no portion of American Jewry seeks to recapture any values institutionalized and expressed in the characteristic experience of the immigrant ghetto. Nor, finally, should it be surprising—however little gratifying we may find it—that the first attempts to set up American Jewish ideologies are based on a rather empty, almost defiant optimism about Jewish survival in the Diaspora and a somewhat boastful confidence in the values we will yet produce.

The question of anti-Semitism also looks different when viewed from an American perspective. In the past, to be sure, American Zionists and anti-Zionists have divided ideologically in their reactions to anti-Semitism almost entirely in relation to the nationalistic anti-Semitic movement of Europe. The anti-Zionist view was that, even if the Jewish status of Emancipation liberalism was inadequate, Jewish ideology must have as its premise the full confidence that anti-Semitism must and will disappear in a new Gentile society. The Zionist premise was that modern nationalistic anti-Semitism would not disappear, and that where it had once appeared Jewish life would increasingly become intolerable.

But the characteristic fact about America was that modern nationalistic anti-Semitism had not really appeared here. Moreover, the usual historic grounds for its appearance were lacking. The Jews in America did not come out of a medieval Ghetto through an act of emancipation, to find that, as a bourgeois people, they aroused nationalistic anti-Semitism. They filtered out of an immigrant ghetto not as a people but individually. They encountered anti-Semitism in America, but it was not based on a nationalistic reaction, rejecting the emancipation of the Jews. The native American anti-Semitism encountered here was the old perennial anti-Semitism in which Herzl discriminated the elements of "cruel sport, of common commercial rivalry, of inherited prejudice, of religious intolerance." This was a kind of anti-Semitism which neither Zionism nor any other modern Jewish movement could or would understand. It was the type of anti-Semitism with which only the medieval Ghetto had provided a certain established basis of understanding.

It is true, on the other hand—and very significant—that European anti-Semitism was able to extend its influence across the Atlantic and demonstrated on numerous critical occasions that the fate and destiny of American Jewry were intimately connected with the fate and destiny of European Jewry. But at other times, the global threat to the Jews having subsided, the American Jews who busied themselves with the matter were faced with the problem of their own, specifically American anti-Semitism.

This problem never really became an ideological issue between Zionists and non-Zionists in America any more than did the problem of American assimilation. At most there was a difference in the degree of concern about native anti-Semitism between Zionists and non-Zionists, a sort of temperamental difference rooted quite remotely in differences of ideas. The Zionist attitude, at bottom, assumes anti-Semitism to be ineradicable. With nationalistic secularist anti-Semitism, Zionism once hoped for an understanding through divorce. But where anti-Semitism remains theological, demanding perpetuation of the Jewish Exile till the Second Advent and the subjugation of Jews to Christians in the meantime, Zionism has no understanding to propose. Thus the characteristic attitude of American Zionism to this problem—that is to say, to native American anti-Semitism—is not to take it too seriously, to feel that it is essentially a Gentile, not a Jewish, problem. On the other hand, it is characteristic of non-Zionism to take precisely this problem seriously. Non-Zionists are inclined to turn a blind eye to the seriousness of nationalistic anti-Semitism such as we saw in Europe, rejecting the notion that Jews should attempt any "understanding" with Gentiles through emigration. The basis for this attitude is an underlying belief that anti-Semitism is not really a "modern" movement, with more vitality and contemporaneity than the Emancipation of the Jews, but only a medieval survival that should expire with the inevitable increase of rationality. Among the "missions" which non-Zionism has proposed for the Jewish Diaspora, one taken up with great earnestness in every country, and in America as well, is to cure the Gentiles of their vestigial anti-Semitism and so to consummate fully the Jewish Emancipation. But whether this is at all conceivable, assuming that Jews remain a distinct entity in the Diaspora, is a problem the new Zionist ideologists still have to face.

The crucial difference which has been brought about in the Jewish problem in the past generation is not only the rise of the State of Israel, but perhaps even more the destruction of European Jewry. This is a factor whose significance is likely to be overlooked because it is a negative factor—and one, of course, which it is anything but pleasant to remember. Without European Jewry, the face of the Jewish problem as it appears to American Jews is radically altered, and in a way simplified. Hitherto, views on the Jewish problem, in its two aspects of assimilation and anti-Semitism, were based on our European traditions and, no less, upon our involvement with the European Jewish situation. But now we live in a Jewish world where, essentially, we see only two main constitutents: ourselves—American Jewry—and the State of Israel. In Israel, the Jewish problem of assimilation and anti-Semitism does not exist, or only in the most indirect and transmuted forms. It continues to exist for us. But the problems of assimilation and anti-Semitism must now be approached in the forms native to America, without the overtones of significance previously lent them by their involvement with the developments in Europe. That simplifies the situation considerably.

We cannot say as confidently that it clarifies it as well. The nature of the Jewish problem characteristic of America has not yet been considered with the degree of rigor and incisiveness that were typical of our European ideologies. That was natural so long as the American situation was regarded as an atypical and not too significant variant of the Jewish problem. It now becomes the major exemplification of that problem in our times. That fact requires, as it is beginning to produce, a new focus in the direction of Jewish thought.

The American
Jewish Problem

THE GENERAL PUBLIC usually takes for granted a simple conception of the way that immigrants are assimilated and "Americanized." This view holds that the older settlers have established an American Way of Life, and the new immigrants, after going through a "ghetto" period when they shed their outworn Old World customs, need only adopt it as their own in order to become real, free and equal Americans. In principle, moreover, the American Way of Life is open to change; it encourages the free expression of individuality. Hence, the fact that certain established ways enjoy a "constitutional" status in America when the immigrants arrive need not prevent the newcomers from influencing future development in accordance with their own individuality. Once they have "caught up" with the already achieved results, they may, if they can, become leaders in determining the new directions American institutions will take. They may even succeed in "naturalizing" some characteristic institutions of their own immigrant heritage. The only thing ruled out, in principle, is to try to lead America back to characteristically "Old World" institutions.

But these principles merely set a problem. To solve it obviously requires some pragmatic test to determine whether any immigrant custom, institution, or cultural manifestation is a legitimately American expression of individuality or must be condemned as an Old World remnant. There is, indeed, a tacitly understood rule of thumb: if any group of newcomers is not ashamed of a public display of its folkways or Old World loyalties, and, particularly, if such publicity makes other Americans familiar with them and they even learn to appreciate them, then they become authentic features of the "American scene." But anything which is closed off and private—any collective intimacy shared only by those of the same immigrant origin and not basically accessible to all others—is stamped as Old World clannishness. Such separatism is certainly permissible in the immigrant ghetto, but it signifies an unwillingness to be "integrated" into the real America.

If a process of cultural selection is actually in effect, there must, then, be something in the nature of a "general social consensus," which passes upon the "Americanism" of novelties and differences. In democratic America, all citizens are equally judges of each other's cultural and institutional offerings, and (as in an election) the rough balance of their appreciation or disdain determines the degree of acceptance or rejection of any novelty made public in the American panorama. Yet the equality of all judges is an equality affected with a difference. The "Old Americans" have an established position which places them almost always in the box seats, rarely, if ever, on the platform of this popularity contest.

To be sure, innovations and new departures are frequent among the Old Americans themselves, in view of the loose and open character of American culture, both frontier and urban. We have only to think of American religious revivalism and denominationalism, of Joseph Smith and Mrs. Eddy, of writers like Poe, Melville, Whitman, Hawthorne, of Henry James or Henry Adams, of our political antipodes from Jefferson and Hamilton to William G. Sumner and Eugene V. Debs, in order to appreciate the range and intensity of variation in our native culture. But in accepting or rejecting these home-grown innovations, it is the Old Americans alone (including those whom they have adopted into the inner circle of "native sons," but not the immigrants and other probationary and neophyte Americans) who determine the consensus. For the values which become institutionalized by their approval form a sort of privileged or nuclear core in the American Way of Life. These are the values that make a serious claim upon the intellectual and emotional adherence of *all* Americans. The jury which approves them must be a blue ribbon jury, made up entirely of such elements as are fully and authentically American.

When some immigrant novelty makes its public debut in America, it rarely claims such serious attention or presents itself immediately to so august a jury. Immigrant cultures get their first encouragement to feel at home in America right in the ghetto itself, for immigrant America is made up of neighborhoods and enclaves where Poles and French Canadians, Swedes and Germans, Slovaks and Hungarians, Jews and Irish and Italians all meet. They meet "marginally," and at first, perhaps, only to clash. But soon, too, they begin to appreciate and enjoy each other's differences, particularly, of course, those differences which are easiest to enjoy and appreciate.

The first critical step in the "Americanization" of a whole immigrant group (rather than of individuals, who begin at once by acquiring the English language and other American ways) is taken when it begins to distinguish between those parts of its traditional culture and institutions about which it need not be shy or ashamed, which in fact other Americans (beginning with immigrant neighbors but ending perhaps with the Old Americans themselves) enjoy watching, and other parts of its heritage which ought better to be cultivated in the privacy of the original group. One can readily understand that it is often the lighter, more superficial and entertaining traits that are easiest to display, that sometimes self-mockery is the quickest way to become popular, while what is most serious is also often most intimate, and best kept private. This rule seems to apply with greater force the more the new immigrants differ from the old established stock.

One could probably set up a status scale for various groups in America according to whether they present themselves to the general public in a serious or a facetious vein. Cultural traits and institutional habits which first succeed in amusing one's immediate neighbors may, of course, eventually enter more or less fully into the approved way of life of even the oldest settlers. Thus, jazz is as clearly a part of the American Way as Yankee Puritanism, and grand opera, Wagner, and Irish political organization are phenomena that are taken more or less seriously by a broad cross section of the population, not only by the immigrant groups who first brought them to America. Yet it still remains true that some Americans, the old settlers, feel so integrated with the American Way of Life that it is precisely their most intimate and serious preoccupations which they identify with our native "public philosophy," that underlying, nuclear social consensus upon which this country is believed to stand. Others, however, in particular the new immigrants, feel that in their more serious and intimate collective expressions they stand apart and are different.

The "Triple Melting Pot"

The social philosophy native to America presents two major opportunities for the recognition of privacies, including what we may call collective privacies.

One such possibility, of most concern to the Old Americans, is suggested by the maxim that a man's business (by which we usually mean also his home and his family) is his private affair: upon this principle are maintained the various social segregations that still characterize us, in spite of American egalitarianism. The other possibility offers immigrant groups a shelter for the cultivation of what is most serious and intimate in their culture: it is the recognition of religion as a private affair, through the separation of Church and State.

It is now well recognized that the ethnic traditions and loyalties of immigrant groups have been most effectively fostered and preserved by the institution of religious privacy. One writer, Will Herberg, has given this observation a very far-reaching and positive formulation. According to Herberg, America has not one melting pot, but three melting pots, or (to quote him precisely) a "triple" melting pot, for the Protestant–Catholic–Jewish division *legitimately* limits the scope of American assimilation. "By and large to be an American today means to be either a Protestant, a Catholic, or a Jew."[1] It is inherent in the American Way of Life that everybody should be one of these, but any one of the three will serve the purpose as well as another. The three religious compartments of America share certain unformulated postulates constituting a general "American religion" and consequently they bear a certain family resemblance to each other. Nevertheless their difference makes it possible for Americans to maintain spheres of serious and intimate spiritual concern in which they are separated. As a result, certain immigrant traditions not made public and general to all America may find a legitimate place on the American scene within the recognized sphere of privacy provided by the church. This, in fact, is the "really American" way in which quasi-ethnic differences may survive even beyond the immigrant ghetto.

But it appears from Will Herberg's analysis that all religions, or at least the three "major" religions, Protestantism, Catholicism, and Judaism, stand in the same relationship to the American Way of Life. Such a conclusion would be a serious error. In fact, each of the three is related in a characteristically different and not necessarily equal manner to the American social consensus.

It is in Protestantism and its typical attitudes and patterns of social organization, even including the social framework of the private realm of religion, that we have the most authentic prototype of the American Way of Life. Religion may, indeed, be a private affair, and all religions are entitled to be tolerated: Mohammedanism and Buddhism and, for that matter, even the "religion" of atheism no less than Catholicism and Judaism. All these have a legitimate (though in some cases a potential rather than actual) place in America. But as for the Protestant religious framework, with its open, voluntaristic sects and denominations, and the freedom of movement from one to another as men move from village to town or country, or up the social ladder—to be fully and truly assimilated into the real America is to be part of this. Jews, Catholics, Moslems, Buddhists, who, when the occasion arises, cannot find their place in a Methodist for lack of a Baptist congregation in any village where they live, or in a Presbyterian for lack of a Congregational church in their town, are somehow outside the most authentic America.

In the view of Protestant America—and who can doubt that this is the most prevalent, the most characteristically American, view?—the freedom of worship, the privacy of religious conscience, is a right of individuals and not of collective entities at all. According to the dominant Protestant and American conception, religion really resides in the individual, and in his direct confrontation of God and of God's Word. The church or the congregation is, at bottom, more of a social convenience, an instrument to help the individual realize religion, than the actuality of religion. Because of this way of looking at the matter, the most characteristic American attitude finds it natural for social distinctions or other personal considerations to determine which denomination or sect a person belongs to at a particular time and place. To change churches rather frequently during the same lifetime is no flaw in piety, for piety is essentially something that occurs within the individual himself, irrespective of a particular social framework. Indeed, the capacity to exercise piety in any one of a number of denominations, according to one's changing circumstances or personal predilections, might almost be considered a positive American trait: it combines complete public mobility with a privacy completely individual in a way very congenial to the American Way of Life.[2]

The American ideal of proper social organization is not that of a totally unstratified, unsegregated, and undifferentiated society, but of a society with class differences and segregations that are loose and permeable, open to the passage of individuals who prove their worth. Assimilation, in fact, is regarded as a process of testing the achievement of newcomers in acquiring whatever is necessary to being a good American; and in order that this test be effective, it is essential that the barriers behind which the real Old Americans entrench themselves should be maintained at the appropriate graded heights—each in turn not too high, yet not too low. Ideally only a man's intrinsic worth should count in his rise to the inner circle, where success in business would be paralleled by belonging to the fashionable church and sharing the other intimacies of the best American society.

To the extent that the Old Americans refuse to respect this ideal pattern in their behavior, they feel vaguely guilty of offending against the American Way. But when immigrant groups, for their part, employ the separation of church and state as a shelter for hierarchical and clannish enclaves of *collective* privacy, the Old Americans cannot regard this as true to the authentic American tradition. The persistence as a solid block of the Catholic and Jewish minorities, even after they have emerged from the immigrant ghetto, means that they stop short of full integration into the American Way and hence, also, into its nuclear social organization.

That is how the Old Americans must necessarily view the matter. Not that this conclusion implies that anything need be done in consequence. Freedom of religion includes, of course, freedom to have one's own idea of what religion really is. If the Catholics regard religion as inhering essentially in the whole believing community, not the individual communicant, and if Jews really believe their religion to occur in their historic community, not to the isolated individual, then such views are no doubt legitimate in America. Nevertheless, they are somewhat foreign to the authentic America. The practical conclusion to be drawn from this may perhaps be summed up in a fleeting reflection that, while the social and economic discrimination practiced by the Old Americans against Jews and Catholics is certainly un-American, in a way, the Catholics and the Jews themselves "invite" it. A certain ambivalence results in the attitude of Old Americans to the assimilation of newcomers. On the one hand, the maintenance of collective privacies is a regrettable aberration which must be permitted under the freedom of religion; but, on the other hand, they, too, welcome the segregations which it sets up in American life, since this relieves them of the pressure that a fully consistent adherence to the ideal of free individual mobility would bring to bear upon their capacity to absorb newcomers socially.

Catholics and Jews have their own theories of what the American Way of Life is, or should be, but it is clear enough that these are largely argumentative and persuasive in character, rather than calm and barely formulated assumptions, like those of the Protestants. Between the Catholics and the Protestants there is this much consensus: while religion is, of course, completely free and private in America, so that all religion must be tolerated, it hardly needs stating that America is really a Christian country. Beyond this, the Catholics would like to convince America that its Way of Life not only permits but should encourage a variety of churches, even to the point of a publicly sponsored segregation between one group of Americans and another. To this end, they argue that the rule against an established church does not really mean that *no* church should get public support, but that *all* should get *equal* support. Whether or not the language of the Bill of Rights bears such an interpretation, it obviously challenges the accepted conception of the American Way of Life. To give formal recognition to permanently segregated religious groups in America would contradict the ideal of religious social organization that is most authentically American, namely, the Protestant pattern of free, open, voluntaristic sects and denominations.

There is, then, no clearcut consensus on what kind of social organization is appropriate for the exercise of religious freedom in America. Against the dominant Protestant view, most congenial to the native American tradition, the Catholics, with their numbers steadily increasing, oppose their own conceptions. As for the Jews, what is most characteristic is that they offer no third conception of their own as a challenge to the Catholics and Protestants.

In some respects, the dominant Jewish tendency is to be more "Protestant" than the Protestants themselves. For example, Protestant enthusiasm for the secular public schools, as an expression of the strict doctrine of separating church and state, only sprang up in the period of Catholic mass immigration. In the face of the segregated parochial schools preserving immigrant differences, the public school began to seem an important instrument of Americanization. But it is the Jews who today most consistently favor the principle of the completely secular, religiously neutral public school. Jews frequently find themselves defending the basic Protestant position against Protestant infringements, such as the presentation of Gideon Bibles or the observance of Christian ceremonies in the schools. On the other hand, there are some

Jews, particularly among the Orthodox, who lean toward the Catholic rather than the Protestant model for religious social organization in America. One finds some support for Jewish "parochial" schools and a readiness to think of a plurality of established, or at least recognized, American religions— including, of course, the Jewish religion.

While wavering cautiously and defensively between the rival Protestant and Catholic conceptions, the Jews are prominently represented in efforts to persuade everyone concerned that not the differences, but the "consensus" among all parties is most significant and most authentically American. In that "consensus," of course, Jews include their own basic beliefs and thus lay claim to being, also, authentically American. The divisive tension in this area of social relationships is apparently disturbing enough so that any formula that would construct a positive "consensus," where nothing more actually exists than an agreement to disagree, becomes attractive to all Americans. The Jews, not involved fully on the side of either party and, at bottom, in fear of both, have, consequently, had great success in their persuasive endeavors. Where else in the world is it so common to speak (not only among Jews but among Christians) of the "Judeo-Christian" ethic, the Judeo-Christian tradition, or the Judeo-Christian foundations of our national Way of Life? This phrase has successfully projected an image of the Jews as an authentic component of the American culture, not just as a religious belief enjoying toleration like all others. Buddhists and Mohammedans are also entitled to toleration, but by no stretch of the imagination could anyone conceive of their claiming to be an integral part of the American Heritage.

To be sure, there is a greater affinity and historical connection between Judaism and Christianity than between either Mohammedanism or Buddhism and Christianity. But this affinity and connection applies to the whole of Christendom (and for that matter, it applies equally well between Jews and Moslems) while the "Judeo-Christian consensus" is proposed as something intimately related to the *American* Way. The proposed relationship is pointless to the extent it is true, and becomes false as soon as it attempts to be pertinent. It is true that Judaism is the root from which arose both Christianity and Islam, and, in its development ever since its two sister religions branched off, it has remained in close contact with each. It is true, too, that American Protestantism, in its reaction against "Papism," was fond of recalling Hebrew origins. But the point at issue is really this: to what extent does Judaism provide principles for social organization in Christian countries, and particularly in America; and, even more important, to what extent are Jews as a collective entity recognized as so essential to the American Way of Life, or to the "way of life" of any Christian country, that their absence would be inconceivable, or would involve a radical alteration in its character?

We need only put these questions to be certain of their answers. In all Christian countries, and in America too, Christian tradition regards the Jews as a people rejected of God, who must eventually disappear when God lets them be reconciled to Him. In the meantime they exist as a people under a ban, who should not be molested, but who are fundamentally alien in the Christian world. Their doctrine, too, is a rejected doctrine, superseded by the New Testament. Consequently, whatever influence "Hebrew ideas" had on social organization, it could not have been through the rejected doctrine of Judaism but solely through Christianity. As for Jews themselves, it is hard to see how their absence from any Christian country, including America, would alter its way of life in any essential.

We come to another difference between Jews and Buddhists or Moslems in America: the latter are not sufficiently numerous to make the need to tolerate them any more than an abstract American principle, while Jews are a concrete, actual component of America. But what, actually, is the social position of the Jews in America, as it must appear from the authentic American point of view? The Jews do not propose a formula boldly and consistently defending the segregation of religious groupings in America as the Catholic ideology does; indeed, by emphasizing the *Judeo*-Christian roots of the American tradition, they stretch the American "consensus" of religious belief far beyond the point where the Protestants can take it seriously. But in actuality, the Jews, too, are far from willing to accept the completely mobile and open organization which, in the Protestant view, is implied in the American Way of Life. Far from recognizing religion as a strictly individual matter, they, like the Catholics, use the freedom of religion as a shelter for their own zone of *collective* privacy. Indeed, in one respect they go much farther than the Catholics, for the Jews alone use the freedom of religion to maintain what is indubitably the tradition of a historic nationality.

For an accurate understanding of the American Jewish problem, it is essential, as we have noted, to trace it to its specifically American conditions. We must understand American Jewry in terms of its difference from other, and specifically from Continental, Jewries. But at the same time, the most essential element of the American Jewish problem is the way in which Jews are different from other Americans. For in America, too, the Jews have to cope with a specific Jewish situation, and it is essentially the same as underlies the Jewish problem everywhere.

The "Protestant community" in America contains certain varieties of belief which include practically none of the Christological elements rejected by Judaism. Yet Unitarians and Universalists, even Gentiles who have no religious belief whatever, fall easily into the pattern of the open, voluntaristic Protestant religious organization, where the nature and quality of piety remains a matter of individual conscience and consciousness. It is not precluded that they attend a local Protestant church on necessary social occasions, particularly on the most intimate ones, such as marriage. But it is not normal for a Reform Jew, or for an irreligious Jew, to attend even such an institution as a Christian Community Church except as a guest. For him to exceed these bounds would mean breaking through an "attitude barrier" that would take him quite out of the range of the Jewish community. A Jew, who may share with a liberal Protestant not only basic religious (or irreligious) ideas but the ideal of an open, mobile social relationship, nevertheless behaves more like a Catholic, who differs sharply not only from liberal Protestantism but from the Protestant ideal of social organization.

44]

But the source of the American Jewish problem is something far more serious than simply the confusion which might
arise from this incongruity. It springs from the fact that the
community the Jews maintain under the shelter of religious
freedom is in actuality the continuation of a single historical
nationality, the Jewish people. All other immigrant churches,
though they may help to preserve elements of various ethnic
cultures, serve also as a zone of partial merger and assimilation of the original ethnic entities. In this respect the
Jewish religion is different from other American churches,
but is fully identical in its social and historic function with
Judaism thoughout the ages, in every clime and condition.[3]

The Catholic Church in America served as a focus and
shelter for Irish patriotism, for Italian folk culture, for
instruction in the French, Polish, and Spanish languages and
traditions. The Lutheran Church allowed Germans and
Swedes to foster their national traditions and aspirations in
America. But let us note the following facts: first, not all the
Irish, French, Poles, or Latin Americans are Catholics, nor
all Germans and Swedes Lutherans—consequently, the ethnic
feelings which the Church helped keep alive were shared by
Americans not included in the tight ecclesiastical community,
but participating in the general American cultural and religious mobility; second, each of the Christian churches contains a plurality of immigrant groups—consequently, while
inhibiting movement beyond the church lines (so that traditional values are kept private and preserved), the church
enables interchanges between immigrants of different origins
within its bounds (so that traditional values are made public
and merged); third, that the long-settled, fully integrated
Old American community itself contains representatives of
all the major immigrant Christian churches, and that an Old
American is quite able to convert, let us say, from Presby-
terianism to Catholicism (as did Orestes A. Brownson or
Clare Booth Luce) without breaking contact with the nuclear
American community and entering into a social segregation.

The reverse of all this is true, of course, of the Jews. To
adopt another religion means, in America as in any other
Jewish situation, to break ties with the Jewish community.
To convert from another religion to Judaism means, in

America as in any other Gentile situation, to break one's old ties and enter into the Jewish segregation. There is only one ethnic group, only one historic nationality, in the Jewish church: it is the Jewish people. The zone of collective privacy guarded by the freedom of Jewish religion is that same culture and tradition shared by all Jews everywhere and at all times. Each Jewish group in its own specific circumstances also shares the basic situation which defines the Jewish problem everywhere: the situation of exile and fundamental alienhood.

The image in which American Jews best like to think of themselves is as an equally authentic component of American civilization with the Christians—hence the popularity of the "Judeo-Christian" tag. At the very least, American Jews think of themselves as a third partner, together with Catholics and Protestants, in the American Way of Life. Such a description of the American "consensus" serves as a useful public relations formula for veiling basic differences, and, for this reason, it has had significant general success. Nonetheless, at bottom, the only Way of Life with a real claim to being established in American tradition is the American Protestant Way. The Catholic ideology may challenge it on the strength of large and increasing numbers, though this challenge is still the challenge of a dissenting minority. But among themselves the various Catholic ethnic groups share the pattern of the "authentic American Way of Life," with its openness and mutual permeability, to an extent that Jews cannot and do not. They are open to assimilation with each other; while the Jews have no one but themselves to assimilate and be assimilated with.[4] They remain, as they came, unassimilated.

Jew and Negro: the Classic Minorities

Hence, if American Jews are to be compared with other religious groups in America, there might be more point in comparing them with the American representatives of Oriental religions rather than with Catholics and Protestants. But the most enlightening comparison, both for similarity and for contrast, is with the Negroes, the other major unassimilable community in America.

Thanks to the immigrant ghetto, the general looseness of social requirements, and the collective shelter provided by religious freedom in America, the New Immigration from Europe was not transformed into a uniformly fused mass in the second or third generation. American experience has taught us to distinguish between "assimilation" and "acculturation," between a social amalgamation that enables the individual to move freely throughout the range of a society and a cultural initiation that only introduces him to its symbols of communication and other conventions. Cultural absorption usually begins sooner and progresses farther than social. But despite the rapid American acculturation of immigrants, our melting pot is still full of lumps, culturally as well as socially. To be sure, the lumps are generally new clusters, formed by dim forces of attraction and repulsion out of elements of the old, which have been subjected to a far-reaching process of reduction. We may still have Catholic or Lutheran ethno-religious groupings which go to make up our common America, or even Slavic-Catholic, Latin-Catholic, German-Scandinavian Lutheran and other, similar amalgams. But we do not, in general, have a rigid continuation of the original groups who came here.

Jews and Negroes—together, perhaps, with American Indians and Orientals—remain more or less alone above the flux that has produced these groupings. The lines that mark out Jews and Negroes remain distinct—and effective. They do not yield to the trend toward fusion and coalescence in new and larger groupings, formed with cognate ethnic entities. These *are* no such cognate entities for Jews and Negroes, because the racial line and the religious bar which mark them off from other Americans are in both cases unique and distinct.

Thus, the Jews and Negroes have been able "to pass," as individuals, only through a harsh process of conversion or dissimulation. Moreover, barriers set up by non-Jews and non-Negroes against the processes whereby individuals may "pass" establish invidious discriminations against all Jews and all Negroes. Other minorities, too, are discriminated against

[47

in consequence of their difference and newness, but, being able to assimilate with cognate groups, they have a certain scope of free mobility.

Similar as the Jews and Negroes are in this respect, there is a sharp difference between the grounds of their identification. The color line is an objective and unalterable barrier, with regard to which no choice is open to the Negro. A man is or is not colored, regardless of his preference. His segregation on this basis proceeds quite simply and automatically, and hence "naturally," as far as the white world is concerned. The problem of "passing" arises only for a marginal few whose color is white or indeterminate.

The situation is quite different for the Jews. Nothing, it seems, could be more subjective, more dependent on personal choice than religious confession. Nothing, moreover, should be harder to detect, if unavowed. "Passing," therefore, is an escape which seems in principle to be open to every Jew. It is a particularly simple affair, one might be led to believe, in any secular democracy practicing the separation of church and state. If religion is a purely private matter and the real basis of society is mere citizenship, as the Constitution might suggest, then the closed circles constituted by churches should circumscribe only partial segments of society and enclose only part of human interests. There should be a wide area of interests in which Jews can meet and merge freely with Gentiles—even Christians. Besides, as secularization makes deeper inroads among Jews and Christians alike, diluting and dissipating faith in both camps, there surely seems no reason for the emancipated ex-Jews to be unable to "pass" freely in the circle of the emancipated ex-Christians.

Yet, even in this situation, unbelieving Jews find that "religion" is a subtle but firm barrier to their "passing." It is not enough for a Jew to lose his religion in order to become a Gentile, even though there may be non-Christian, or rather, ex-Christian, Gentiles. For mysterious reasons, it seems that a Jew must become a Christian before he can become a Gentile—and even then, transformation is not completed in his own generation, but only in his progeny. Paradoxical and enigmatic as these facts may appear, they are nevertheless an accurate empirical report of the situation.

The fact of the matter is that religion plays a far greater role in shaping the structure of our society than is indicated in our secularist, democratic constitution. The barriers which traditions rooted in religion have set up against the social intermingling of irreligious Jews and Gentiles are almost as formidable as the color bar between Negro and white. Although large numbers of both Jews and Gentiles have only the slightest connection—or no connection at all—with church or synagogue, the accepted standards of conventional respectability are still those of religious tradition. Thus, a Gentile, himself passed beyond piety, is still a part of Christian society, just as a *"poshea Yisrael"* (a sinful Jew) is still regarded as a son of the Covenant. Moreover, the irreligious Jew and Gentile both respect the restrictions which their religious communities conventionally impose on familiar relationships with outsiders, for they must do so on pain of endangering their own family and community ties. And it has proved a severe shock to many a sanguine Jew to discover how strictly those conventions confine his freedom of movement among Gentiles. The evanescent and, in his eyes, incongruous line of religion proves almost as rigid as the palpable, unalterable line of color.

Though the objective effect of the "religious" bar is almost identical with that of the color line, its subjective effect is far more complex. Just as the objective effects of the color line are brute fact, so the inhibitions of white men against free intermingling with Negroes appear as elemental, stark unreason, as arbitrary as a physical fact and equally independent of any justification. For the whites, this means that the inequality and segregation of the Negroes is merely a defect in our civilization, not a contributory element in our higher culture. It is not only that the generally accepted principles of democracy and religion are opposed to the way we treat Negroes. No defense of these practices has become a positive element even of rebellion in our culture. In spite of the feeble efforts of a few Southern philosophers in pre-Civil War days, no serious attempt at an intellectual or artistic justification of Negro disenfranchisement and economic suppression has left a permanent impress in our heritage from history.[5] We should have to examine the cruder operations of the subconscious to find any remote and devious influence of Negro suppression upon American cultural creativity. Essentially, Negro-hatred is nothing more than an element of vulgarity in American culture.

On the other hand, the Negro, too, is painfully blocked from finding any cultural value in his condition of segregation. After generations of effective separation from African roots, efforts at recovering aboriginal themes which would appear to the American Negro as profoundly his own must seem artificial and prove abortive. Even the elements of song, poetry, and religious culture which have flowered in the segregated Negro community of America, not to speak of the characteristic Negro folkways, are spoiled for sensitive Negroes because they scent in them the sour odor of merely compensatory activity, more truly expressing the oppression of the whites than the free creativity of the blacks. It is for this reason that the dominant, and almost exclusive, cultural impulse of the Negro community in America is to break the wall of segregation and to enter fully into a society existing on the basis of the culture of Christianity and the Bill of Rights, for this is the only intrinsically valuable culture that the Negro knows. Tendencies to build up an individual cultural tradition of the Negro, and hence to find positive values in enforced segregation, are weak, and consequently tend to be eccentric and sterile.

Both Jews and Gentiles among American liberals discover with difficulty how different the situation is with the "Jewish problem." It is only against considerable inner resistance that emancipated Jews and Gentiles realize how intricately the Jewish-Christian conflict is involved in the higher culture which they both share—and which subtly sets them one against the other. Anti-Jewish attitudes are not merely vulgar lapses among Occidental Gentiles. They are woven into the warp and the woof of all that is most precious and most intimate in Western civilization. The symbols of the eschatological war between Church and Synagogue adorn cathedrals and inform the catechism with high dramatic tension. The awe and dread of Ahasuerus, of the Cain people, have contributed to the beauty, the sublimity, the pathos of the whole range of Western religion, folklore, poetry, drama, music, art. It is in Shakespeare's Shylock, Dickens' Fagin, the power of the Oberammergau Passion Play; it is in Chaucer, in Grimm's fairy tales, in the great chorales of Bach—and even in the queerly ambivalent Jew-apotheosis of Leon Bloy. Nor is it something a Gentile can escape by "emancipating" himself, by becoming a liberal or a socialist —or, obviously, a fascist.

Thus, every Gentile must find out, if he questions himself ruthlessly enough, that his difficulties with the Jew are not merely the arbitrary consequence of the conventions of a churchly society to which he belongs not by faith but by social inclusion. At some point, he must begin to realize that, though his best friends may be Jews and though—as far as his personal life is his own entirely to govern—he may meet them individually on the same terms as any other friend, nevertheless there is in his personal culture a rejection of Jewishness, a tension directed against it which cannot be dismissed as no more than a vulgar lapse.

The situation is perhaps even more complex for Jews. Having become "emancipated," they soon feel obscurely aware that they have engaged themselves to a Gentile culture which, to be sure, in its highest expressions often accepts them fraternally (as it does the Negroes), but at the same time, in other respects of its highest expressions, fundamentally and passionately rejects them. In sharing this culture they are called upon to reject themselves, to cast off their Jewishness not merely as a misfortune—a view many of them would enthusiastically endorse—but as a sin. Many, indeed, are the Jews who submit to this demand, and for this reason spread the insidious type of self-hatred common, in concentrated or diffuse form, among Jews. This self-hatred is not merely the reflex of a frustrated drive toward assimilation, as among Negroes, but directly expresses an acceptance of the fundamental anti-Jewish bias of Gentile culture.

Even among Negroes, where the situation is much simpler, the attempt to "pass" implies a renegadism towards one's own kind. For, after assimilation, the white-skinned ex-Negro must pretend to have white prejudices at least to the extent of listening unprotestingly to the slurs habitually uttered against blacks by uninhibited whites. A Jew can "pass" too only by a conversion—or a pretended conversion—to fundamental anti-Semitism.[6] Two reasons make the renegadism this implies particularly odious. First is that when a Jew "passes" he does not usually do so in silence and in concealment, like the Negro, but by a public pronouncement. He must let everyone know when he renounces the Jews and accepts Christ. The second is that the anti-Jewish bias which a Jew adopts in "passing" is a far more elaborate and intellectually cogent system of ideas than vulgar Negro-hatred. The Jew who converts has, often enough in Jewish history, become not only a missionary to the Jews but an outstanding Jew-baiter. As a result of this history, powerful and widespread attitudes of suspicion and contempt for renegadism and apostasy pervade the Jewish community. These attitudes persist even among those who no longer believe either in the Jewish or Christian versions of providential history. They were strengthened, in the generation which saw the rise of Zionism, by new experiences which showed how assimilation even into Gentile movements of secular protest could involve the Jew in complicity, before or after the fact, in greater or less degree, with popular Jew-hatred and its effects.

These considerations close the road to "passing" for many Jews who no longer take either the Jewish or Christian side in the quarrel between the two eschatologies. Yet even among Jews who never dream of abandoning their community, the anti-Jewish bias of the Christian culture of their environment has become widely accepted. The depreciation of Jewish culture and Jewish tradition in comparison with Christian culture is not by any means confined to converts, whether cynical or sincere.

The suicidal anti-Semitism of Otto Weininger[7] represents this specifically Jewish self-hatred in full self-consciousness. In attenuated forms it leads many Jews, far from suicidal, to view Jewish tradition with Christian prejudice, as outmoded. But among others, the demand to turn from themselves with a holy hatred causes rebellion, and even a strange warmth in their memories of their Jewish past. How this can happen even beyond the threshold of conversion is illustrated in the following confessional statement by a Jewish Catholic proselyte.[8]

"In the course of time I became a Catholic. As I stepped into the green pastures of the Church I became a freak, a Jewish convert. By now there should be enough of us not to be museum pieces. But still, everywhere I go with my Catholic friends, I am pointed out as a Jewish convert, isn't it wonderful. Except for a handful of people, I have never been treated as anything but a Jewish Catholic. Now, I would like to be treated as neither the one nor the other but as myself. My background and my faith are part of me. If I went to a priest for spiritual direction I was more often than not told that I had to break my 'Jewish pride' or that since every Jew was antagonistic and aggressive, I had to face it within myself and tear out these seeds of Satan. If I settled into a group of Catholic friends, someone new would come along and I would be introduced as a Jewish convert, isn't it wonderful. It is not wonderful. If a Jew becomes a Catholic, it is not because he wants to mend his 'Semitic' ways. It is because the fear of Hell enters into him that he leaves the familiar life he grew up in and goes into a cold and strange new way of life. It is not wonderful, it is very necessary for some people."

This girl tries to defend herself against the projection of her individual conversion into the historic setting of the conflict between Church and Synagogue. She resists the awareness that she has not abandoned a nothingness for a something, but has chosen between two sets of values which have powerfully striven against one another through endless ages. Even though she remembers Jewishness as "familiar" and perhaps "warm," in contrast to "cold and strange" Catholicism, she would prefer to think of Judaism as a triviality which could stand in no serious opposition to Christianity. Her attitude, strange as it seems in a Catholic convert, is similar to that of those Jews who strive to pluck the nettles from the rose bush of Jewish-Gentile brotherhood by eliminating references to the Synagogue of Satan from the catechism, or doctoring the mystery of the Jew's share in the Crucifixion so that it becomes harmless. *They* would like

[53

to reduce the Christian opposition to Judaism to a triviality.[9] They little reck how Herculean—nor how thankless—a task they have undertaken. For the antagonist is everywhere, and he has laced the accumulated treasure heaps of two thousand years of Occidental culture with a million explosive charges.

But there are others, too, who still take up the gage of battle every day cast before the Jews by the Gentile culture which they hoped to make theirs. These Jews are almost morbidly analytical of their own motives. They do not hide from themselves the fact that if the Jews have existed for so long, it is not because of some mechanical blockage in the historical machine which consumes nations and tribes. They know that Jews have existed because their Jewishness is, after all, a world of values which they cherish. Among "emancipated" Jews this awareness sometimes assumes rather grotesque shapes—as in the claim that precisely to be "emancipated" is to be essentially Jewish, so that Gentile ex-Christians who somehow fail to provide Jews with an environment capable of assimilating them are, if they only knew it, really—or ideally at any rate—Jews. This is the source of many protestations that democracy is really Jewish—or Judeo-Christian— or that the "alienation" of the uprooted intellectual is a *mimesis* of a pattern set by Jewishness.[10] Among more integral Jews, the awareness of the values of Jewishness takes more natural forms, continuous with the ways of all Jewish history: as in Zionism, or the efforts to maintain or "reconstruct" the Jewish community in the Diaspora as a distinct entity.

The Negro problem stems from this fact: they are being oppressed because of a social situation for which there is no cultural justification and into which they can read no cultural significance. The Jewish problem comes from a quite different difficulty: they are afflicted by a social situation to whose justification both Jews and Gentiles have devoted some of their highest cultural endeavors; but history has taken such a turn (not only in America, but throughout the modern world) that these cultural significances have been obscured, attenuated, and, for many, lost.

Out of their different situations, the Negroes and Jews have come to adopt different basic approaches to a solution.

As the Negro situation is brutally clear and blunt, so his response is positive, bitter, and unequivocal. But as the Jewish situation is often vague and tenuous, so their responses are confused and ambivalent.

The most drastic expression of both the Negro and the Jewish problem is, of course, in the hatred of whites for Negroes and of Gentiles for Jews. We have noted that the two phenomena differ most curiously, and this, in turn, leads to sharply different responses. Anti-Negro feeling in America is almost entirely devoid of cultural justification, being a purely vulgar impulse; but, at the same time, fear and hostility toward the Negro is a theme that occupies a central place in the political history and in the evolution of the national conscience of this country. Anti-Semitism, on the other hand, never emerged as an issue of importance in our political history or in the revolutionary and ideological struggles that shaped our national Way of Life; but, in the context of general Christian culture, which is a profound source of America's highest values and traditions, hostility to the Jews is a central and pervasive theme.

The Negro, then, is faced with hostility and discrimination in the most unmistakable form; it arises as a perennial political issue; and it is squarely opposed both to the only system of culture that he himself can possibly accept and to the true culture of America. Facing such a challenge, the Negro necessarily responds with great bitterness, yet with a consistent, simple, and increasingly bold program of action. His battle line is clearly drawn (wherefore his morale is high): he must compel by law and moral pressure what the white world ought to grant under the very principles of justice and charity by which it professes to live. It is true that the full measure of what the Negroes necessarily seek—integration into white society—may involve not only conscience, which may be compelled, but the gift of love, which can only be freely granted. But the difficulty of the Negro aim in no way blurs its simple clarity or beclouds its elementary rationality. For there is that in love, too, which seeks to be compelled, and our common humanity is certainly a fitting reason to compel it.

Anti-Semitism in America is not and has never been an important political movement. It faces the Jews in America not in parliamentary or judicial forms, nor chiefly in a definitely organized shape or in activities which challenge an equally definite response. Moreover, its roots, not specific to America but common to all Christian countries—and, for that matter, paralleled wherever Jews have lived among Moslems—reach into a terrain of ultimate religious disagreement, a zone where Jews and Christians find themselves holding to opposed values that neither can relinquish, because these antitheses form the justification for each one's very existence. To be sure, the claim for love and tolerance among all God's children holds even when the siblings are radically opposed in their understanding of God's Word. But such a claim for love and tolerance must somehow find itself compatible with renouncing the demand that fundamental anti-Semitism be abandoned by the Christians. For no Jew, once he faces the question, can fail to understand how inconceivable it would be for a Christian to remain a Christian if he had to give up his belief that the Jews are a people rejected of God.

The lack of a politically significant anti-Semitism expressing itself in terms of the national history, together with the pervasive presence of popular anti-Semitism deriving from Christianity, makes the Jewish response anything but bold and clear. There is no "clear and present danger," no tangible threat of specific character to give us the objectives, and instil in us the morale, for defensive battle. We have only the pressure and the threat of such a perennial anti-Semitism as is essentially inseparable from Christianity itself. Would we, even if we could, seek to extinguish together with its source this menace that hangs over us? Such a possibility was precluded from the moment the Jews realized that they could never hope to convert the Gentiles; hence, that they were in Exile.[11] The whole significance of Exile to the Jew is precisely that he cannot even wish to extinguish the basis of hostility to himself, because it is a hostility inherent in the very existence of the world he inhabits. To judge the world is a judgment that none but God and his Messiah could conceivably encompass.

In a time when Jews were attuned to Exile as to their own spiritual milieu, a standard form for the solution of this dilemma existed—the ghetto. In establishing this and similar forms of segregation (despite the antitheses that are part of any situation relating the powerful to the powerless), there was a certain consensus between Jews and Christians. The segregation and subjection of the Jews went together with an understanding that the Christian Church and authorities would keep the "hostility-potential" of fundamental Christian anti-Semitism under such control that Jewish life would be at least tolerable.

In America today (as, for that matter, in all secularized societies) we lack the prerequisites for a Jewish-Christian "understanding" regarding the state of Exile. There is not even a real tradition of the ghetto here, for the immigrant "ghetto" we know of is something altogether unrelated to the *permanent* status of segregation, subjection, and alienhood which this word historically signified. But in any case, even in European countries with a ghetto tradition, modern secularism has made a new Jewish-Christian understanding through ghetto institutions an impossibility. The modern attempts at a secular revival of the anti-Jewish tradition which, in a religious society, was held within limits and under control through such institutions as the ghetto led to the unlimited Jew-hatred of racism. In other countries, where modern, nationalistic anti-Semitism has not been significant, fundamental religious anti-Semitism remains, in principle, a private affair, in spite of the public effects that it may produce. Particularly in America, with its Protestant ideal of the individual conscience as the sole arbiter, and the individual consciousness as the true subject, of all "religious experience," there can be no public understanding regarding a status for the Jews based on the idea of a collective Exile. The American Jews, like Jews in all countries where public life has been organized on a secular, non-traditional basis, have consequently lost, or been led to repress, their sense of Exile. Having seen anti-Semitism rejected by history as the principle of the Jewish public status, relegated to the infra-public realm of popular stereotypes and the private realm of religious culture, Jews in America also have an underlying awareness that fundamental anti-Semitism has thereby been loosed from institutional control; and our historic folk wisdom tells us through innumerable examples that a static popular prejudice can be transformed into a dynamic popular impulse without any essential change in its nature. Owing to our uneasiness about this very fact, the idea of the Judeo-Christian consensus, whose functional utility in the general community we have already noted, has become very popular among Jews. It serves as a placebo for ourselves quite as much as a prescription recommended in the art of public relations for removing the source of our anxiety.

Compared with the Negroes, the American Jews have had to face only the most insignificant expressions of hostility. Yet one cannot fail to note the striking contrast between the high morale and mounting confidence of the Negroes in facing enmity, with the evasiveness, uncertainty, and unresolved anxiety of American Jews in the face of anti-Semitism. The reasons for the difference, however, seem quite adequate to account for it. The Negroes meet with a hostility which is specifically American, and quite definite and open in its nature—despite the subtler overtones of a global color conflict which occasionally complicate it. Their growing confidence arises from their success in defeating the adversary in successive historic encounters, in the feeling that the tide runs their way. But what the Jews sense is that their adversary, having no specific place in the particular American scene, really confronts them in a global conflict; that the threat is not definite and perceptible, but so pervasive and so perennial and of so protean a character, that they do not know how to grapple with it. There is anti-Semitism in America, but it is endemic rather than epidemic in form, sociological rather than historic in context. One effect of increasing Jewish absorption in their local American situation could be, perhaps, to dull their intuition not only of Exile, the specifically Jewish situation, but of the anti-Semitism with which it is inseparably coupled. But it is impossible for Jews to live, like the Negroes, almost exclusively in terms of their American situation. Even the kind of animosity with which we are faced, precisely because it is not specifically American, cannot but make us continually aware that we really live in a global, perennial, specifically Jewish situation quite as much as in a local, contemporary, specifically American one. Even on a conscious level, the American Jewish concern over anti-Semitism is not expressed solely in the defensive assertions of a Judeo-Christian consensus. It also shows itself in our continual watchfulness lest endemic anti-Semitism after all turn epidemic, and our constant dread that unorganized popular prejudice may become organized, here too, as a historic national political movement. It shows itself in our immediate awareness that wherever *this* threat arises today, whether here or in any other country, it is aimed against us all. But, beyond this, in the fringes of our consciousness there is always the folk wisdom of our people, warning that we live in a world which is by its very nature hostile, and that there is always danger where the endemic popular antagonism to us is not under institutional restraint, but is allowed to take the form of a free-floating animus, subject only to its own impulses.

The Invisible Ghetto

With respect to social and economic discriminations, the American Jews have had to suffer very little indeed in comparison with the Negro. Here, too, the Negroes face a blunt and brutal oppression, to which they can respond in a positive and unambiguous way. The Jews, however, are under social and economic restrictions whose forms and effects are involved and ambivalent. In the case of the Negroes, the true consensus of religious culture between themselves and the whites allows no particular complications to arise from this quarter. Among the Jews, the whole significance of their social and economic segregation is complicated by their cultural dilemma.

The economic and social disabilities from which Negroes suffer represent a constant flagrant oppression. The economic and social restrictions which Jews experience in America become serious only under special conditions, and are always accompanied by some show of justification. At the present time, certainly, the Jews of America stand as high as, and possible higher than, comparable groups in material well-being. As relatively new immigrants, they might be expected to rank somewhere below the national average in income and status. In fact, they already are above the average in this respect, having prospered more than other groups who arrived together with them, more even than some who arrived somewhat before them, and being outranked only by the Old American groups.[12] This prosperity is not without its darker side, psychologically at least. For to Jewish intuition, it rings an alarm signal whenever an opinion poll shows how significant a part of American Gentiles feel that Jews are too rich or have too much power in this country.

Jews experienced a true and palpable social and economic oppression only a short while ago—in the immigrant ghetto. A major part of adult Jewry in this country today still remembers the cold water tenements of the ghetto slums, the grinding poverty of families whose immigrant parents had suddenly transformed themselves into factory hands and whose sons grew up in the anxious days of the Great Depression. American Jewish economic historians are fond of pointing out that while Jews made truly remarkable advances from the squalor of the ghettos, they actually followed closely the dominant trends of growth in the American economy at large. Whatever occupations and ecological areas were expanding, wherever new industries were arising, there the Jews, just breaking out of the ghetto, were among the first to be found. Thus it was by becoming naturalized and typically American that the Jews became prosperous. But this very fact hides what upon analysis turns out to be an effect of social and economic restriction; and it also bears within it very troublesome implications for the position of American Jews, present and future. For beneath the heartiness of prosperity there is still the nagging awareness that a well-being which depends on an expanding economy and the alert exploitation of its opportunities may not be secure, either economically or socially. A boom can always burst. But to the younger generation now growing up all these fears are almost totally strange, and if the sustained prosperity of this country continues we may find (despite the difficulties still experienced in entering medical schools or getting special post-graduate medical training, or the problems some kinds of engineers still face in finding employment with companies in their field) that crude economic disabilities have practically disappeared as a component in the American Jewish awareness of the Jewish problem.

The same cannot be said of social "discrimination" and the subtler economic restrictions associated with it. For there is a reverse side to the statement that Jews followed the same trends of occupational change and economic advance as the whole expanding American economy. Stated in other terms, this means that Jews found themselves excluded from positions and opportunities already established by the Old Americans and other earlier settlers, and thus were "forced" to make a place for themselves in new occupations and in new industries that arose in the rapid growth of the country.

The same barriers, of course, faced other immigrant groups, and if the Jews made more rapid progress than others it was because their background had predisposed them to the attitudes and given them the basic skills for participating in the not yet institutionalized and incorporated advances of the American economy. They had a bent toward the new urban clerical occupations, the service trades and free professions, salesmanship and promotion—and, emerging from the immigrant ghetto, each man on his own, the Jews readily ventured into such experimental industries as the movies in their infancy, or, in our time, electronics, plastics, or the new pharmaceutical industries. Other immigrants, who came from a peasant background, were far more likely to make a slow advance from unskilled to skilled labor and so on up; so that the Jews naturally outpaced them. The Old Americans, on the other hand, had the advantage of social and cultural background and family ties, so that in most cases they could find a place in well-established and secure corporate structures. Hence, they could afford not to become involved in the newer and more risky branches of the American economy unless they had an individual taste for venturesomeness, or to enter these fields only after enough had already been ventured by others to make buying in an attractive risk.

The Jews not only burst forth into the mainstream of the American economic advance. The explosiveness of their progress was also related to what they burst out of. For the momentum of the Jewish rise in America reflects the energy with which Jews rejected the immigrant ghetto. Those city

[61

slums were sad enough places for all the immigrants who had come from villages and semi-rural towns in Europe. But for the Jews there was an additional cause for the feeling of being pent in. The Jew was traditionally used to being his own man, and whatever the proletarian ideologies that flourished in the ghetto slums, the sons of the immigrant generation broke out of the ghetto with a fierce impatience to put behind them all that reminded them of their parents' dependent economic status. Jewishness itself was among the qualities which the aspiring young men often felt as a drag upon their flight toward the beckoning horizons of the real America. The second generation of Jews in the ghetto was like a thick crowd in a confined space that had suddenly become noisome: there was an irresistible surge towards the exits.

It was a somewhat unexpected and ironical outcome of this break for freedom when the second generation, emerging from the immigrant ghetto, found themselves once more bunched together, segregated from the real, authentic nuclear America. How this came about is easy to understand, but it was certainly unexpected and not entirely welcome to those who experienced it. Social restrictions blocked many occupational outlets from the ghetto, and the predisposition to seek independent commercial and professional occupations, rather than the skilled trades usually open to immigrants' sons, still further reduced the available number of exits. If so many young Jews were all trying to run away through the same doors, it is hardly surprising that they found themselves together again outside. Moreover, an area of "second settlement" which the first Jews (or any of the other new immigrants) succeeded in penetrating was soon left to the newcomers, as the old settlers, keeping their social distance, withdrew from it to new residences. Socially, at least, the flight of the second generation turned out to be that of the swarm rather than of the liberated individual, and it led to no significant assimilation in the strict sense, however great the acculturation these American Jews had undergone.

To all outer appearances, the resettled second generation Jews were thoroughly Americanized: in speech and dress, on the job and at play, there was hardly anything to distinguish them from other Americans. But the Jews soon enough became sensitized to subtler cultural differences, that existed, to be sure, for every other second-generation American group but nowhere in such a sharp and ineffaceable form as for the Jews. Of course, in acquiring the common culture of America, no immigrant group lost every memory that was brought over from the land of its origin. In addition to the general American medium of communication—the language, gestures, inflections, allusions, and mannerisms in which the fashion of the day had caught up the precipitated essences of local history—each second-generation group retained traces of its ancestral accent, expressions, witticisms, folkways and folk loyalties, its Saints' Days and ethnic celebrations. These traces of difference had passed the test of public display, and whatever mockery had first greeted them had now, by a double accommodation—of the immigrant culture to the American norm, and of the American standards of appreciation to the immigrant novelties—been modulated into a show of fundamental acceptance: according to the classic formula, America now "smiled" when it said "mick" or "wop" or otherwise noticed vestiges of ethnic difference. Accepted symbols had been arrived at for acknowledging these facts as a public part of the American scene, in which all Americans shared by a mutual understanding. These differences were now the occasion for backslapping rather than for jeers —or polite avoidance.

Such signs of acceptance are particularly important for Jews—in view of the social and economic composition of their community—in America, as elsewhere in modern, secular society. The second- and third-generation American Jew increasingly depends on his ability to sell, and in order to succeed, he must be able to sell not only his product but himself. The Jew, in outstandingly high proportions, is an entrepreneur or a professional who seeks a market. Moreover, at the peak of his success, security and recognition depend on his acceptance by the established corporate structures at the very top of our economy and society. All America, we are told, is more and more having to sell itself, whence the growing dominance of the "other-directed" personality;

[63

and it is natural enough that a Jewish sociologist has perceived this most clearly.[13] For Jews not only exhibit an unusually high proportion of occupations that require the ability to sell oneself, they also encounter peculiar difficulties in accomplishing that very feat. Every rising Jew eventually discovers that there are Jewish differences which can never occasion the hearty slap on the back, but at best evoke the chill of a polite avoidance. For the most persistent Jewish differences are also the most serious. They are, moreover, the differences which are shared by Jews everywhere and which everywhere set them apart from the world they live in.

The basic Jewish difference is a difference with non-Jews in the conception of what has been the divine plan of world history. It is, so to speak, a difference of the calendars by which the whole rhythm and time perspective of life is governed. Diaspora Jews all live in cultures which place them in a historical perspective determined, for example, by the Christmas and Easter holidays, while they themselves continue to observe Simhat Torah and Passover and Tisha B'Av as though everyone recognized they were God's favorites. European "revolutions" in medieval and early modern times, from the Cluniac reforms of the First Crusades to the Germany of the Religious Wars or the England of the Roundheads, were all more or less religious in nature, and whatever changes they brought about in the national character of Italians and Frenchmen or Germans and Englishmen had little bearing on the question of the Jews.[14] But the French and American Revolutions, and most recently the Russian Revolution, attempted to set up national calendars replacing or supplementing the religious ones. To this secular life rhythm and historic perspective Jews could apparently acculturate, since the specific differences between the Jewish historical view and the Christian were simply ignored and everything seemed to start out again on a clean slate.

So it was that many Jews during the era of civil emancipation came to believe that the quarrel of the Jews and Christians over calendars could be ended, that neither Saints' Days nor High Holy Days had any relevance to the ordinary business or social relations between Jews and Gentiles. But they were profoundly wrong. These things are not merely topics of debate between two sets of clergymen. They are rather the language of converse of the two social groups. To carry on their business or ordinary social relations without recourse to these languages, without the gestures, expressions, habitudes which in a Jew are offensive to a Christian and in a Christian are insulting to a Jew, involves a strict self-discipline not to perform habitual or colorless acts because to the other party they are not habitual and thus have strong emotional color. It involves, further, the creation of a sign language or an inexpressive special lingo for the restricted spheres of intercourse of ordinary social and business relations. With this restricted lingo there always remains something vital unexpressed, hidden, undisclosed, and perfect understanding is thus in principle not possible.

Without a common language of allusion and reference in which to carry on business affairs and ordinary social relations, there is always distrust and hypersensitiveness: the danger of being either naively credulous or insanely suspicious. Between two such different backgrounds intercourse is carried on without humor, good sense, understanding. Jests and bargaining tactics cannot automatically be discounted and taken easily in course, and since the two parties do not understand the tentativeness or the seriousness of the proposals made in the others' language—things "instinctively" perceived by persons brought up in the same language and habits of social action—there is always a great unease about dealings between strangers.

And "strangers" the Jews remain, however close to the nuclear, authentic America they may come. The crowning acceptance is one they can never attain so long as they remain Jews. We, too, inhabit the "invisible ghetto" of which Herzl, not yet a Zionist, wrote in his play "The New Ghetto." For no matter what differences may be caused by the diverse histories of the countries where Jews live, there is, at bottom, one and the same Jewish problem that confronts them all in the modern, secular, Westernized Diaspora: it is the age-old Jewish problem of exile and alienhood, complicated, however, by a lapse in the transmission of our ancient culture which gave it all significance.

The problem of Jewish alienhood presents itself in a particular form to the second generation American Jew. He had fought free of the immigrant ghetto—but far from having entered the authentic core of America, he found himself in a new, invisible ghetto. He knew, of course, that this peculiar twist of fate had something to do with his Jewishness. But he had dropped so much cultural luggage in his escape from the ghetto that he had very little idea any longer what Jewishness —and particularly *his* Jewishness—really consisted in.

From many sides, there are pressures upon the native American Jew to seek to rediscover his Jewishness. There is first of all the brute fact that a Jewish community, or at least a Jewish aggregation, persists beyond the immigrant ghetto. This in itself would make of Jewishness and the Jewish problem no more than a true analogue of the Negro situation in America: it becomes a sheer existential fatality, or, as Heine put it, an *Unglück,* a misfortune. However, the Jews can never take the same clear line to their "misfortune" as the Negroes so naturally take to theirs. The most indifferent Jews remember the tradition of Jewishness as a matter of divine election, and if there is any inclination today to regard it as a decree of blind fate, this cannot fail to appear as a degeneration of Jewish consciousness. Moreover, the American Jews are always aware that their "fate" resembles all too well a self-chosen destiny, for they are a community constituted fundamentally by belief. Even if the choice that keeps one in the Jewish community is no more than the unwillingness to go so far as conversion, it is by an implicit choice that a Jew remains a Jew. There is, then, upon every Jew an implied demand to justify to himself (and by his conduct, to the world) his choice to be a Jew.

The American Jewish community of fate turns out, moreover, to be a fate not too difficult to bear. It is a company of men and women of a fairly high level of general well-being and culture, and of recognized respectability. If one were thrown into such company by nothing more significant than making a five-day voyage across the Atlantic on the same ship, it would be natural to let a common rudimentary shipboard culture develop, if only in the form of entertainment. How much the more natural to seek common values in an aggregation like the American Jews, whom the Gentile world willingly regards as a natural group precisely in their capacity as a recognized religion. Moreover, while many in the second generation may put up with being Jewish as a triviality of fate, it is not possible to justify such a status to one's children—unless, of course, parental self-respect is another value one no longer takes seriously. The great majority of American Jewish parents naturally take a different attitude, and since their offspring are bound to be Jews, willy nilly, they would like to give them some form of Jewish culture to make them like it.[15]

A "revival" of Jewish religion and Jewish culture has obvious social utility in such a situation. Since Jews must live together in the same house, Judaism can serve as a cultural décor to make our collective home liveable, giving it an individual style for those within, and its representative symbols, the synagogue and the rabbis, can present an acceptable facade for the world outside. This statement is flippantly phrased, perhaps, but in substance it is far from being a travesty of the facts. Judaism and Jewish culture are being subjected to drastic revision in contemporary America. There are many Jews who look to Judaism to justify their collective existence but are totally unable to appreciate it directly; for this requires scholarship, or at least a pervasive atmosphere of scholarship accessible to every individual Jew. That is something American Jewry does not even desire to achieve. But what is needed with urgency is to present such extracts of Judaism as can reconcile the Jews to their fate and make them proud and happy in it; and considering the general Jewish ignorance and Hebraic illiteracy of the American Jews, obviously the externals of the tradition are what make the first appeal. That these externals have Jewish authenticity—this only the rabbis are educated enough to determine; and of this they serve as symbols and guarantees.

It is not surprising if the "Jewish culture" promoted by this situation bears an unmistakably American aspect. Religion is, of course, a privileged realm of privacy in America, and consequently is under no compulsion to submit to the test of publicity and the taste of the general consensus. But the Jews themselves are a public for whom Judaism must be made attractive, and they are mostly without the Jewish literacy needed to appreciate their own authentic culture; and often enough they are so estranged that they have lost their feeling for its style. Consequently, the externals of Judaism are subject to rather rough alteration to suit their taste. Other causes place the *ideology* of Jewishness, too, under a compulsion to Americanize. For Judaism also appears as the public facade that the Jews present to America. Consequently, there is the tendency to present the essentials of Judaism in such a selection and emphasis as will underscore the "Judeo-Christian consensus," with its peculiarly American importance.

All this tends, naturally, to render somewhat awkward the central place held in Jewish tradition by such ideas as exile and alienhood, and the distinction and chosenness of the Jewish people. Even the existential fatality by which Jews continue to exist as a community in America seems more like a mild witticism of the *Weltgeist* than a stern decree of any serious divinity. But there are occasions when American Jews are awakened to a meaning of Jewish fate and a sense of Jewish destiny that are of the highest and most exigent seriousness. The catastrophes that have befallen world Jewry in our time affected us as our very own; and in the struggles of world Jewry for independence in Israel we knew our own destiny to be at stake. Moreover, the Jewish fate and destiny revealed to us in these extremities threw into sudden focus the ultimate meaning of those fatalities and challenges presented to us in such fuzzy outline and subdued tones in our special American situation. We became aware of the underlying serious meaning that being a Jew has always had in history.

In the same way, it is impossible to live forever in the synagogue only as in a socially useful institution. At some time one is bound to realize that this professes to be the House of God. How, one must ask, do I stand before God? Do I really belive in Him? Do I believe in Him as a Jew? It is in such questions of conscience that the Jewish problem must arise for American Jews.

These questions, usually muted, nevertheless cause a constant unrest in the minds and spirits of American Jewry. In one form or another, also, they underlie the various attempts that have been made to provide ideologies for Jewish life in America.

Secular Solutions
of the Problem

IN DISCUSSING SOLUTIONS for the Jewish problem today, it is necessary to take account of the radically changed situation that has resulted from the rise of the State of Israel. Whatever else may be in doubt, it is clear that one essential element that characterized the Jewish problem until recently has now been eliminated. The Jews are no longer a universal minority, everywhere dependent. In Israel they are an independent majority.

What this has altered, first of all, is a certain fundamental obligation that was felt by every Diaspora Jew. The Jews as a dependent minority were a people always on the defensive, and their millennial survival appeared not only to themselves but to the whole world (whatever the esteem or contempt in which the Jews were held on other counts) as a supreme demonstration of doggedness and courage. Martyrdom is a kind of virtue whose meaning the Jews first demonstrated to the world, and a title which their history earned again and again.

But a time came when to many Jews the reasons for being martyred lost their meaning. Their Jewishness reduced itself from a Covenant known in clear and compelling terms to an incomprehensible fatality: they were Jews because, for some unanalyzed reason, the agreement they had made with the Gentiles, to bypass the Jewish-Christian quarrel through a compact of civil equality in a secular state, failed to be carried out according to their anticipations. On the European Continent, where Jewish emancipation ended in successive crises, many Jews could see no more in their Jewishness than a misfortune. In America and other countries where emancipation was smoothly achieved, the significance of Jewishness was reduced still further, from a misfortune to an inconvenience, at most. But both in Europe and in America, Jewishness persisted, and in its persistence repeatedly brought to consciousness the essential historical identity of Jewish fate throughout the world. Thus, no matter how senseless the fact of being a Jew might seem, biographically considered, there always existed for every Diaspora Jew the consciousness of a historical character in which he was clothed: no martyr himself, perhaps not even fit to be a martyr, he stood as the contemporary representative of martyrs and heroes.

This was a patent of nobility, no matter what distortions and grotesqueries went with it; and this nobility implied unquestionable obligations. Whatever the reasons for being a Jew, it meant one was the heir of men who had borne their destiny bravely. Hence, their manner of being a Jew was a standard against which one could not help being measured and measuring oneself. To be a Jew meant, also, being part of a universal minority which, everywhere dependent, was in many places abused. This, in turn, presented a constant challenge to stand or to run, to take part in mutual defense with one's brothers under attack, or to abandon the common cause in order to seek one's own safety in hiding. It meant, lastly, that the continued survival of the Jews—of a collective existence whose defense the whole world agreed had been heroic—now had no other defenders than oneself, and other Diaspora Jews like oneself who shared in the misfortune of Jewishness. Consequently, even if one could conceive of any country's really accepting an offer to surrender the Jewish position (which involved effectively absorbing all the Jews, a test none had yet shown itself able to pass), the Jews who carried out this surrender would have to judge themselves, and be judged by the world, as cowardly and weak successors to their ancestors, and as treacherous renegades to their brothers who had no such option.

To change all this was one of the most characteristic aims of Zionism, particularly of the Zionism of the West and of Herzl himself. No sooner was Zionism proclaimed than it opened a new prospect to men who were Jews only out of inscrutable necessity or out of a sense of shame: it gave their Jewishness a positive meaning, demanding courage and enthusiasm, for it offered them anchorage in a clear goal in the future, rather than in a half-forgotten past demanding piety alone. But besides, when the aim of Zionism was accomplished, and the whole world recognized Palestine as the Jewish National Home, this would provide a radical solution for the dilemma of non-Zionist Jews too, who now were saddled with obligations for a heritage they no longer wanted, or, if they tried to escape this fate, were liable to their own and the world's judgment as deserters of a desperate cause. With a State in which Jews would constitute an independent majority, the Jewish people could survive on a normal, mundane basis, and no longer depend entirely on the loyalty of Diaspora Jews. The Jewish State would offer to "non-Judaist" Jews two options: if their loyalties had been fully engaged in the Zionist movement, they could come and live in the new Jewish State, where all kinds of Jews, of whatever shade of belief or disbelief in "normative" Judaism, would constitute a free Jewish entity; if not, then the existence of the Jewish State would relieve them of the sense of shame which the idea of abandoning Jewishness in its insecurity had always evoked, and remove this barrier to their assimilation.

The State now exists—and it has had the promised psychological effect. At least, it has certainly had it among the most articulate of those whom, by their own account, nothing but a sense of honor and obligation bound to the Jewish people. Arthur Koestler was among the first and the frankest to avow that the success of Zionism had made him free to assimilate, and, he felt, it should have the same effect on many more who were in his position.[1]

Thus, one of the effects of the rise of the State of Israel has been to bring into focus again a "solution" for the Jewish problem that is perennially appealing, but quite as regularly shown to be illusory: the assimilation of the Diaspora Jews. It is, of course, incorrect that a sense of obligation was ever the sole cause which bound any Jew to his community. As we have already shown, not only other underlying questions of conscience but very substantial sociological factors preserved a Jewish community which in America, for example, contains, in addition to Orthodox, Conservative, or Reform Judaists, many Jews not committed specifically to Judaism.[2] Taking this into account, what, then, would be involved in an attempt to solve the Jewish problem by assimilation, if such an attempt were seriously meant, and not merely put forward as a form of journalistic self expression?

A Program for Assimilation

It is really extraordinary how lightheartedly otherwise serious-minded people recommend to the Jews speedy assimilation—a "solution" of the Jewish problem which, among its other defects, happens to be impossible. Perhaps "impossible" is too strong a word. Thorough and rapid assimilation of the Jews is not altogether impossible, of course, but it does require certain very rigorous conditions. It is highly questionable whether most advocates of assimilation have ever considered what those pre-conditions are.

One way of achieving speedy assimilation would be that of Ferdinand and Isabella in the Catholic Spain of 1492: giving the Jews the choice between conversion and expulsion —or, more effectively, death. Jews today might be told to choose between emigration to Israel (or execution) and conversion. Some would emigrate or become martyrs. The remaining Jews would be converted and eventually assimilated. The occasional backslidings and survivals of Jewish rites which history records among the Marranos do not detract from the over-all effectiveness of this Draconian method.[3]

The same effect cannot be achieved by half-hearted measures. Among the very groups who feel that the Jews are not an ethnic but a religious entity, there is often found a rather pathetic yearning for the development of a world religion.[4] This would presumably relieve the persons in question, without requiring the specific act of conversion, of the burden of being distinguished from Gentiles even as members of a religious entity. But even today, doctrinal (and, almost equally, ritual) differences between these Jews and, let us say, Unitarians or Universalists are practically nonexistent. Yet this is not enough to permit intermarriage and free social migration between the two groups. They are still socially divided, owing (as we have seen) ultimately to disagreement about the place occupied by Jews in the divine history of the world. Only mass conversion, even in this case, might make possible the social submergence of one group in the other. Even a merger of the two sides in a new church, based on an agreement to overlook or compromise the question whether or not Jews were rejected by God, would have to be specifically compacted. But the cost of such a new alliance would be severance of the social ties of each partner in the transaction with the respective Jewish or Christian communities.[5] And that would not bring about the assimilation even of the merged groups, let alone of all the Jews. Nothing but outright and universal conversion could accomplish that end in any "Christian civilization."

The rapid assimilation of Jews into a secular community might also be possible, but again only under rather specific conditions.

The first condition would be the fostering of an avowedly non-religious element in the population, until it grew sufficiently large and representative to be more than merely a marginal group. The separation of church and state and the wide dissemination of "scientific" views are not enough to produce such a group. We have seen in this country that, notwithstanding the effects of both factors mentioned above, religious traditions maintain a noteworthy hold on the people—and we still have a "Christian civilization." The non-religious *demimondes,* where unbelievers of both Jewish and Christian origin mingle, can serve to "assimilate" only an insignificant fraction of the Jews. If the task is to be fully accomplished through a secular medium, the expansion of our present agnostic fringe would have to be "fostered" by rather drastic means. Even the governmentally encouraged and state-abetted anti-religious (both anti-Jewish and anti-Christian) campaigns and organizations of pre-war Soviet Russia did not succeed in doing a really thorough job. To

74]

accomplish it would certainly require a greater and more persistent effort. Yet the lessons of Soviet experience indicate certain lines along which the problem of the rapid assimilation of the Jews in a secular society might be approached by any ruler powerful enough and sufficiently interested to do it.[6]

Other pressures would also have to be applied if the assimilation of the Jews were to be accomplished with the postulated speed. It would not be sufficient to provide a non-religious neutral ground of sufficient extent upon which Jews and non-Jews could meet and merge. It would also be necessary to herd both the Jews and Gentiles into the assimilation zone. Obviously this implies first of all—in addition to the vigorous prosecution of an anti-religious campaign—strong measures to repress the prejudices and scruples of both about entering into relations of the requisite degree of intimacy with each other. But it also calls for a thorough and purposive redistribution of the Jews among the Gentiles, geographically, occupationally, and socially.

The mere opening up of careers to Jewish talent does not make for rapid assimilation. If allowed freedom to choose the location, type of work, and social position to which they themselves would aspire, Jews have shown that they will tend to concentrate in large cities or their suburbs, gravitate toward a certain group of occupations requiring specific skills and aptitudes, and find their niche in a relatively restricted and superior range of social positions.[7] The result, a tendency to the concentration of Jews in residence, occupation, and social position, does not promise a speedy merging with the non-Jewish population—certainly not with a broad and representative cross section of Gentiles.

If one were seriously interested in rapid assimilation, he would have to favor a rigidly directed program of retraining and redistributing Jews, in accordance with scatter diagrams of mathematical precision. This would also mean that the acceptance of Jews would have to be forced not only upon a relatively sophisticated and detached portion of the population—the urban, industrialized and bureaucratized elite—but also upon peasants and miners, laborers and clerks,

[75

over the whole length and breadth of the land. As for the Jews (in so far as their voluntary collaboration would be necessary or desired), for them to undertake to solve their own problem by assimilation would demand an occupational changeover so radical that only the kind of idealism shown by the labor settlements in Israel could accomplish it. It would be necessary, in short, somehow to evoke an assimilationist *halutz* movement. But "assimilationism" is a doctrine which pretends to be practical and adaptive rather than idealistic and defiant of circumstance. And it is hard to imagine any people, even so curious a people as the Jews, developing a heroic *ethos* in the cause of its own collective suicide.

We have taken the trouble to paint this picture in some detail not merely as an exercise in the fantastic and repulsive. Ordinarily, one might even regard it as indelicate to probe into the meanings which would rise to the surface if we were to take seriously every suggestion that Jews could contribute toward interfaith understanding by doing away with whatever it is that marks us out as different. There is a certain tacit understanding between Jews and Gentiles in this country (and no doubt in other lands) about such remarks. No Gentile, when he throws out a comment of this sort, dreams of its going any farther than mere talk; so he never bothers to think what the suggestion would actually mean for him, what action it would require. The only function such a suggestion has in conversation is to shift slightly the burden of grievance from the uncomfortable shoulders of the Gentile onto those of the Jew. The Jew, for his part, smiles briefly in a moment of pained silence—and the conversation discovers some new subject. And when *Jews* propose to solve their problem by assimilation, the particular admixture of irony that is proper to such statements is something other Jews are experts in estimating.

Nevertheless, if assimilation is not a solution of the Jewish problem, even after the rise of the State of Israel, it is an increasingly significant part of the problem. For while assimilation may never be able to submerge completely a large Jewish community in any free society (this being a task only religious or secularist totalitarianism could encompass), it does manage to detach from the Jewish community a significant proportion of "marginal" Jews. To such Jews, regarded by themselves and others as virtually assimilated, how to convert their constructive into an actual position or, alternatively, how to find their way back to the Jewish community may seem like the very essence of their problem.

Under American circumstances, with the heightened emphasis on the religious character of the Jewish community, all varieties of secularist Jews are placed in a marginal position by the prevailing fashions in Jewish ideology. Zionism is the sole remaining ideology which can still make the Jewish community meaningful to many secularists, who could now find little relevance in their Jewishness if the founding of Israel really meant the end of Zionism. For the other secularist ideologies which have been proposed as a rationale for the existence of the unassimilated Jewish community in America have long since proved inadequate for that purpose.

Ethnic Autonomy
and Cultural Pluralism

The idea of ethnic autonomy is one of the ways in which Continental European Jewry responded to the crisis of Jewish Emancipation. There were certain obvious conditions favoring such a conception in Eastern and Central Europe which were lacking in Western Europe and America. The Jews in the East were a long-established community who could often trace their settlement as far back as the autochthonous majority groups. Hence they could feel equally entitled with all other subject nationalities in the polyglot empires of Russia and Austria-Hungary to assert rights of cultural self-determination. In the West and in America, on the other hand, the Jewish communities were relatively young or composed largely of immigrants, who in the very act of migrating had implicitly accepted an obligation to adopt a new culture and assume a new nationality.

Nevertheless, the idea of ethnic autonomy was transplanted to the new Jewries in the West and in America almost as soon as it began to flourish in Eastern Europe. It arose in the West, first of all, as a principle regarding the Jewish problem in general. The Jewish problem was thought of by these American Jews in terms exemplified primarily by the Eastern Jewries whose troubles and aspirations they shared as a vicarious experience. This was true not only of the Zionists and other secular nationalists in the immigrant ghetto, but of Zionist liberals and intellectuals who were part of the real America. The stalwarts of the Yiddish press, on one hand, and men like Stephen Wise, Judah Magnes, Louis Brandeis and Horace Kallen, on the other, found in the twofold fight for the Jewish National Home and for national minority rights for European Jewry in the Succession States an ideology of collective rights that they sought to apply to America as well.[8]

From the very beginning, however, it was obvious that any kind of "ethnic autonomy" which these theorists might propose for America would never be as full-blooded an affair as they attempted, at least, to secure for Europe. Obviously, the American Jews never felt themselves at home in America in precisely the way they thought the Jews entitled to be at home in Eastern Europe. As to this, there was no real difference between the ideological proponents and the ideological opponents of Jewish minority rights. The former believed that the maximum possible formal organization and legal authority was necessary in order to preserve the Jewish community and its culture. The latter believed that in the name of adjustment to the era of Emancipation the minimum of organization and authority was desirable. Both agreed, however, on two fundamentals: that, in one way or another, the Jewish community and culture must be preserved; and that in Eastern Europe a far higher degree of formal organization and legal authority was a natural and proper Jewish demand than in the West and, above all, in America.

Thus, the Jews in Eastern Europe, with the approval and support of substantially the whole of American Jewry, demanded (not only in their own countries but at international conferences) the right to maintain autonomous tax-supported schools conducted in Hebrew or Yiddish, as well as other national linguistic rights. Jewish community organization, to a varying extent in all European countries, tended to be centralized and often was able, with government sanction, to levy a tax on its membership. In America no one thought of asking such rights and authority for the Jews here. Demands like these were obviously precluded by the principle of the separation of church and state and other established American institutions. Consequently, just as the theoretical opponents of minority rights agreed to support ethnic autonomy in the special situation in Eastern Europe, where everybody else demanded it, so the ethnic autonomists and cultural pluralists understood it was impossible to demand minority rights for Jews in America, where nobody else had them. In both instances, it was a case of concessions reluctantly made only because objective local conditions refused to conform to the principles each one really would have liked to apply.

In America, then, the position of the ethnic autonomist and cultural pluralist was basically one of trying to swim against the stream, to maintain or to restore the maximum possible cultural continuity and communal integration against the influences of Americanization that threatened to sweep them both away. The difficulty of this task was made even greater because the ethnic autonomists and cultural pluralists were themselves in rebellion against the normative tradition of Orthodox Jewry. They were secularists. They wanted to break the bonds in which they felt Judaism to be strait-jacketed, and let Jewish culture express every deviant tendency which arose spontaneously among Jews. They wanted to open the portals of Jewish culture to the newest thoughts of the world about them. They wanted the tightly controlled organization of the community to be broken and reshaped by the Jewish *demos*. And, finally, they wanted the Jewish people itself to gain such a status and undergo such social reformation as were needed to make it capable of maintaining itself as a secular entity in a secular world.

The Zionists and territorialists followed this line of thought to its ultimate conclusions: since their aim was essentially to transform a tribal religion into a national culture, it required nothing less than a national territory and the reformation of the Jewish social and economic structure from that of a foreign trading colony to that of a self-sustaining people. The ethnic autonomists in Eastern Europe sought to achieve the result with slighter means: through legal guarantees and communal authority. But in America even this much was not available: not only national sovereignty but an established minority status could hardly be dreamed of. The American ethnic autonomists and cultural pluralists had to draw up a program for maintaining an open national culture and a democratic communal organization on no stronger basis than the voluntary support of a community in Exile.

That a noble and abstractly appealing idea is expressed in ethnic autonomism and cultural pluralism can never be gainsaid. A good case can be made out that the underlying conception of these theories is essentially related to the American Idea: both enshrine the values of liberty and individuality, spontaneity and variety. It is the basic kinship of the two systems of ideas that made Horace M. Kallen, the disciple of William James and apostle of cultural pluralism, also become a Zionist and a protagonist of secular Jewishness and cultural Hebraism. Because of this affinity, the fact that conditions do not encourage the realization of autonomist and pluralist ideas in America does not necessarily prove that they ought to be abandoned. There are objective conditions which impede the realization of many aspects of the American Idea, thus causing many an American Dilemma, but we do not, on that account, propose that principles be given up.

It is by no means *impossible* that a "secular" Jewish culture, such as our parental generation knew, should continue to be maintained in America. Yiddish has flourished with particular distinction among the minority cultures in this country and still sustains a considerable literary and social vitality. The Hebrew-speaking and Hebrew-writing circles active in this country are bent upon reproducing themselves, and one cannot safely predict their demise. America is large and free, and if any group or cult is sufficiently determined to make a major contribution of time and energy for the preservation of its idea, there is room for it to thrive.

However, what we have, in this instance, is far more a cult than a culture: it is an artificial growth not natural to our native soil, and it can complete its life cycle, run to seed, and sprout new growth only if a loving hand supplies both fertilizer and topsoil, with no consideration of cost. To maintain a secular Jewish culture in this country would require special social conditions favoring a far greater Jewish segregation than now exists. Such social conditions existed in the America of our parents' days because, as immigrants, their first habitat in America was the ethnically divided immigrant ghetto. In our own, largely native-born, generation which has emerged into America-at-large, religion alone establishes a natural and legitimate segregation of Jews from other Americans. This kind of segregation does *not* provide a natural habitat for the effloresence of a secular Jewish culture. But there is no reason why devotees of Yiddish and Hebrew culture, by gratuitious exertions, should not maintain both the schooling and the type of segregation required to foster Yiddishism and/or Hebraism as American cults.

While not impossible, such an effort nevertheless is hardly likely to continue indefinitely on any significant scale. There is something intrinsically self-defeating about the notion of maintaining a secular culture as a cult. A true culture is in its very essence a natural and free growth, and to cultivate it artificially leads to cramped and distorted expressions without spontaneous appeal. Thus, beginning with the resolution to keep an uprooted culture alive by force of special exertions, one finds that in the end special exertions are again needed to get a public to appreciate its expressions. A natural culture has that in it which captivates its native audience, while a cult must necessarily provide itself with a captive audience. For free artists, this is a fate which even in its triumph is poisoned with the quality of self-defeat.

But secular Jewish culture has indeed turned into a cult, so that not only artists are responsible for its continuance. Both Yiddishism and Hebraism have developed organizations to promote them, and such organizations are always remarkable both for optimism and insensitivity. If the product they promote should become subtly adulterated, it need not cause them to flag in their efforts. They would continue to operate by virtue of their function alone, with no real dependence upon further justification. But they deal with a captive audience, and if their product loses its spontaneous appeal, all the more need to rely on an appealing justification.

There is, basically, only one justification for any system of secular values, whether it exists as an artificial cult or as a natural culture: it must have significance for history, it must know that it has historical reasons, a cause and an end, a source and a goal, it must have faith in its own duration, and above all in its future. A secular cult can long command the enthusiasm and devotion required to foster it artificially only if its adherents can believe that the time will come when their faith will prevail organically, as a natural culture. In short, a myth is required which envisions the triumphant enthronement of the cultists' exotic beliefs over historical society. To come back to our specific example, the cult of Yiddishism in America, which once found a kind of natural habitat in the immigrant ghetto, could thrive over the long stretch and on a significant scale among our own largely native-born generation only if it could successfully propagate the myth of an America-of-the-future based on a federalism of autonomous, secular, ethnic cultures. But we are unable to believe in such a myth for America, and the more we recognize that it is the manifest destiny of America to be culturally federalistic solely on religious lines, the less likelihood of working up popular enthusiasm for the cult of secular Jewish culture in America.

The full-blown ideology of secular Jewish culture, of Yiddishism and Hebraism, the American analogue of European ethnic autonomism, began in the immigrant ghetto, where it had a sort of natural habitat. It never really emerged from the immigrant ghetto into the real America. Today, when that ghetto no longer physically exists, except for insignificant remaining groups, Yiddishism and Hebraism may still persist as cults, but with no real future in America. If any historical myth gives their adherents the courage of their convictions, it is not the idea that America could ever become a country organized as a federalism of autonomous, secular, ethnic cultures. Yiddishism and particularly Hebraism are buoyed up by the morale inspired by prospects still apparently open before Jewish secular culture in other countries: for Yiddish, in Canada and the Latin American countries, and possibly, in one form or another, in Europe and Israel; and for Hebrew, in the rebirth of our ancestral culture in Israel. As long as American Jews continue to become aware that they share a common fate and to be inspired with hope in a common destiny with Jews everywhere, so long will devotees of Jewish secular culture find the courage to propagate their cult. But those who invest a major part of their life and self-expression in such a cult will inevitably cut themselves off, to that extent, from the real America, including its American Jews. They will speak to them from behind the walls of a self-imposed ghetto of the spirit.

In a sense, cultural pluralism represents an attempt to naturalize the concept of ethnic autonomy in the real America. A Jewish philosopher, Horace M. Kallen, is most prominently associated with the rise and propagation of the idea.[9] But it proved best suited for pragmatic application to the situation of non-Jewish ethnic groups who were becoming naturalized collectively in America.

Despite some ambiguities, it is fairly clear where the essential difference lies between the ideas of cultural pluralism and ethnic autonomy. Cultural pluralism demands that the various collective individualities, in expressing their different themes, should jointly "orchestrate" them. This is a demand which never occurred to the ethnic autonomists. The reason is obvious. To "orchestrate" the themes of the various ethnic cultures means to modulate their differences for the sake of a general social consensus. Thus, the idea of ethnic autonomy was "naturalized" in America by accepting the demand of the general American consensus that ethnic communities (particularly immigrants) remain open to mutual influence and, above all, to the influence of the American Idea. Under such general molding (or, as the original ethnic autonomists might say, such "restraint") the individual differences of immigrant groups are transformed by the pluralistic cultural *ensemble* into "contributions" to a total "harmony."

The ethnic autonomists and the cultural pluralists are opposed to the same foe, to cultural imperialism. In Eastern and Central Europe, where the ethnic groups were conscious of their titles of old settlement, the fight was for equal rights of the minority with the majority, the subject with the ruling cultures. The claim was for self-determination through territorial sovereignty or other forms of legal autonomy. In immigrant America, these claims could not be made; for even if one were permitted to keep one's traditions intact in the shelter of tight communal segregation, it meant living in a ghetto, not in the real America. But in giving up segregation in order to become naturalized the ethnic minorities also abandoned any claim to *equal* collective rights in America. For immigrant cultures to become open to each other and to the American Idea meant a renunciation of any claim to equal rights with the established American Way of Life. The theory of cultural pluralism does, indeed, oppose the demand of hundred percenters for flat conformity to Old American patterns and interprets the American Way of Life as essentially receptive to difference and hospitable to individuality. Even so, this very openness constituted a supreme American value; and, in naturalizing themselves, immigrant cultures have to submit to it. Thus, hidden in the proposal for an orchestration of cultures is the idea of a hierarchy of themes in the American symphony, with some dominant and others subordinate.

Cultural pluralism, in actuality, meant that immigrant communities, while adopting the dominant American culture, retained and contributed to America a form of subculture acceptable to the general consensus. The more superficial the cultural differences that immigrant groups brought with them, the easier the naturalization of these differences in America.

The idea of cultural pluralism found some pragmatic application among non-Jewish immigrant groups as they became collectively naturalized owing to the fact that in their more serious cultural values they were basically united, for these values were ultimately rooted in Christianity. Their differences were most striking, as well as aesthetically appealing, precisely where they were superficial. Festivals, folk-songs, dances—all the sensual expressions of popular immigrant culture were those things in which ethnic groups were most individual. In its naturalization, consequently, each group could contribute these easily accessible values to the American symphony (thereby expressing its own "subcultural" individuality) while it picked up the dominant themes of the American Way of Life. United with other native and immigrant Americans in the more profound cultural concerns—to be quite plain, in religion[10]—the immigrant group found within either the Catholic or the Protestant church a setting that permitted at least partial assimilation and ethnic merger with Americans of different historic origins. The orchestration of individual ethnic themes was possible in America only to the extent that they were written in more or less the same key.

Even with regard to non-Jewish groups, the theory of cultural pluralism has its obvious limitations. The American symphony seems properly orchestrated if one listens only to its strictly ethnic themes—always barring the case of the Jews. But the least one can say about the Protestant-Catholic themes in this medley is that they are written in rather different keys.

Cultural pluralism is least of all applicable to the situation of the Jews in America. The externals of Jewish culture are not the ways in which its historic individuality has been most readily expressed. Religious custom itself limited Jewish self-expression in music and the plastic arts, and encouraged the more earnest rather than the more expressive forms of literature. The Jews were forced to migrate too often in their history and were too conscious of themselves as both a wandering and a global people to invest their individuality completely in local customs and folkways, in costumes and manners, or even in the languages they spoke. The most individual expression of the Jewish people is also its most serious and most inaccessible expression: it is the value system most universal among all Jews and most particular to the Jews alone, the Jewish religious culture. This is not a substance easily molded according to the formulas of cultural pluralism. Thus, the ideas of Horace Kallen were doomed

[85

from the start to be basically irrelevant to the Jewish situation, with which he himself is most intimately concerned.

If cultural pluralism has proved irrelevant, however, it is not for lack of effort to apply its precepts among Jews. The attempts to naturalize Jewish culture in America take two forms. Both forms seek, in effect, to make Jewish culture superficial enough to be acceptable, as a sub-culture or as a shared theme, by the general American consensus. One way is to provide Jewishness with a generally accessible sensual surface, using whatever aesthetic elements are available or inventing them where they are unavailable. Thus, the complex regimen of Eastern European religious folkways cannot be fully reproduced here, except in ghetto enclaves, since it involves a whole community freely ordering its life under Jewish Law. Yet, some elements of the traditional folkways can be retained, and these are beginning to enjoy a new vogue, in all denominations of the Jewish religion, as a positive need becomes recognized to give our Jewish community house an individual Jewish décor. In addition, since new customs and new popular arts springing up in the State of Israel—the national dances, songs, and art objects—are, naturally, certified to represent Jewish culture, they, too, come into fashion as a medium for giving a Jewish look to American Jewish community institutions. Lastly, the Jewish community does not fall behind any American ethnic or religious community in encouraging musicians, artists, sculptors, architects, and authors to provide embellishments, in the most modern manners, for our institutions and functions. The very avoidance in the past of so many of these fields of expression by Jewish culture makes it easier for anything done by a Jewish artist, or on behalf of a Jewish institution, to be accepted as valid Jewish culture.

But everyone is aware that Jewish culture is essentially a book culture. Accordingly the second form in which an attempt is made to naturalize it is to present the Jewish religion itself as essentially American. Horace Kallen himself was one of the first to lend some support to such an undertaking. He, like Ahad Ha'am and other secularists who seek to establish Jewishness primarily on a cultural base, participated in the search for a common Jewish essence remaining identical in all the changes of history. Such searches never remain unrewarded, and Kallen arrived at his own definition of Hebraism just as did Ahad Ha'am, or Moses Hess, and many another. Naturally enough, there is a great similarity between Kallen's Hebraism and the Pluralism which he regards as essential to the American Idea.[11] In this, or in other forms, it is fairly easy to construe a basic consensus (or, as in the case of Ahad Ha'am, a basic distinction) between the Hebrew spirit and the spirit of any other community or religion with which it has been in intimate contact, including, unquestionably, America. Nor can anyone deny that at certain abstruse levels all such constructions have some elements of validity. But nothing but superficial generalities can result from an attempt to interpret the *actualities* of life of Jews among Gentiles in terms of such a trans-historical spiritual consensus (or disjunction).

Horace Kallen, himself, is acutely aware of a far more significant cultural and historical context which determines the actual relations between Jews and Gentiles, in America no less than anywhere else. He knows that the root of Jewish difference is something profoundly serious, too serious, in fact, for any conceivable orchestration in harmonies approved by the general consensus. It is none other than the total disagreement between Jews and Christians over the nature of the Jewish Exile.[12] The theme of the rejection by God of His chosen people is, indeed, a "contribution" made, in a sense, by the Jews to American culture, as to all Christian and Moslem culture. But neither do the Christians and Moslems accept the Jewish interpretation of this theme, nor can any Jew (including Jewish secularists) accept the Christian or Moslem interpretation—except by a complete self-denigration.

If Jewish culture, taken not as an abstraction but as a historical reality, has any essence by which it has always been identified, surely this theme of Exile and Redemption must be a central part of it. Moreover, it is the essence that remains as the irreducible experience of being a Jew after everything else in Jewish culture has been abandoned, in the most extreme form of Jewish secularization. Any Jewish secularist must experience it as part of his Jewish problem

[87

to be unable to identify completely with historical Jewish culture, with a tradition that has, after all, been essentially religious. Yet, however little of the content of Jewish tradition a secular Jew may take seriously, he remains a Jew by a sort of implied choice—and, if he is able to analyze the process of this choice closely enough, he knows that he is a Jew, ultimately, because he is unable to accept openly the anti-Semitism implied in virtually all Gentile views of the Jewish place in history.

Even without such an analysis, what a secular Jew is left with after he has lost every other content of Jewish culture is the bare sense of alienhood, without even its mythic sublimation in the idea of Exile. Among the ideologies which seek a "solution" for the Jewish problem in America, one should perhaps not neglect to mention those tenuous, individual rationalizations by which Jewish intellectuals occasionally try to build something upon the sheer fact of "alienation." At one extreme, these views, making a virtue out of fatality, simply assert the paramount value of the individual artist, freed from the bonds and conventions of any community. Whatever a free artist creates, expressing his alienation as in fact a liberation, is justified in its own very being, and it is unimportant whether any community—his own Jewish community, from which he departs, or the general American community, in which he has not arrived —accepts it or understands it.[13] Such a theory, of course, must always remain an individual rationalization rather than a group ideology, since it assumes that the community ends in individual creations, from which there is no feedback to the community.

A more elaborated stage of this idea seeks—but in vain —a community of the alienated among the intellectual elite of America. The alienated Jewish intellectual belongs by birthright to this communion, since the whole Jewish community is itself alienated. The Gentile intellectual in America achieves alienation in his own person by transcending his community. Thus, that the alienated should form a *community* is an idea with more appeal to Jews than to Gentiles. But it was the crucial perception of Jews who leaned to this theory that the community of alienated intellectuals is no real community, so that those who composed it had almost entirely lost the essential human support of a community. And this was acutely felt as a loss . . . [14]

Waldo Frank brings this trend of thought a next step further—or perhaps one should say he stays one step nearer the original idea of Exile from which all such rationalizations take their departure. He demands that the whole Jewish people in Exile take as their mission to be alienated intellectuals, or at least to be a community which serves as a proper environment for the birth and nurture of the alienated intellectuals who are its most authentic expression.[15]

This, to be sure, begins to look like an ideology. It does not dilute the historic idea of communal Exile into the contemporary, individual problem of alienation. Consequently, too, it is able to see the Jewish cultural difference as something like a mission instead of a bare existential plight. But in this way it begins to lose its secularist character and elevates the Exile into a kind of cult. It takes on the character of a religious solution for the Jewish problem, falling short, however, precisely because it remains an individual rationalization, not a reasoned proposal pertinent to the actual problem and aspiration of the community.

Alienhood and Exile are, in any case, the historic core of the Jewish problem which remains to be faced, even if by a secularist approach one has discounted the significance of much else in the continuous tradition of Jewish culture. From this rock-bottom experience of Jewishness two ways lead back to a solution of the Jewish problem: a secular way, through Zionism, and a religious way, through the recovery of faith. But with the rise of the State of Israel it has become more rather than less difficult to face the problem of Exile and Alienhood.

The Dilemma of
Neo-Zionism

The historic success of Zionism has presented an acute intellectual dilemma to American Zionists. Many secularist Jews, before the rise of the State of Israel, gladly accepted the obligation to sustain the existence of the Jewish people by their loyalty and found personal fulfillment in working through the Zionist movement for a political and social-economic solution of the Jewish problem. Such loyalty and activity was the expression of a myth sufficiently pertinent to history, and particularly to the pressing demands of the time, to inspire all the enthusiasm required by a secular cult. But the rise of the State of Israel confronted Zionists (particularly American Zionists) with the urgent need for ideological "reorientation."

That the American Zionists are in a severe intellectual and moral dilemma is so obvious that it is practically bad taste to mention it. Not only non-Zionists but other Zionists as well, particularly the Israelis, challenge them with pitiless insistence either to go to Israel and build it, or give up the name of Zionist. This is a choice that is not easily made, nor can an American Zionist feel that the demand to choose between alternatives so formulated is really justified. He feels in his bones that there is a third way, *his* way; but he rarely goes very far in trying to define it, because the grounds he stands on are shifting and insecure.

We are all familiar with the theory American Zionists are building in self-defense.[16] America, they say, is not Exile, but a home to which we cleave. We are a fully integrated community here, in no danger of liquidation, and with no thought of emigrating. Yet, they insist, we are Zionists. What constitutes our Zionism? The answer, if familiar, is vague. Hardly old enough to have been fully formulated, it has already acquired the blurred outlines of banality. What makes us Zionists is the doctrine that the Jews throughout the world are One People.

What exactly does this imply and why is it a belief that makes Zionists different from non-Zionists? That Jews are One People—the very premise with which Herzl began—used to mean primarily that Jews have a common history and destiny, and only secondarily that they are united by common cultural bonds. Thus, the first thesis a fledgling Zionist learned to defend against opponents was that "Jew" was an ethnic rather than a religious category. "Common history and destiny," in the old days, meant the Jews lived everywhere "in Exile," or as a "minority" in all countries, and would never be secure until a Jewish State was established. Now that the State exists, a continuation of this stress on our common destiny leads naturally to demanding that American Jews join the migration to Israel. If we reject this, we are forced to play down the idea of a common Jewish destiny as a specific Zionist doctrine. (Even non-Zionists in America are fully aware that a threat to Jews everywhere is a threat to us, too, and that the strength of Israel is of vital interest to us, too.) We are left then with our common Jewish culture as the main feature of our "distinctly Zionist" idea that Jews are One People.

This culture we share particularly with Israel. And here the American Zionist turns at bay and becomes aggressive. In our debate with the Israelis, we deplore and view with alarm tendencies which we discern in Israel to discard the common cultural heritage that unites them with the Jewish people throughout the world. As Zionists, determined to maintain Jewish identity in the Diaspora in perpetuity against all the winds and floods of assimilation, we demand of Israel that it be more *Jewish,* so that it may become our spiritual home and help us to live—away from it.

We have come a long way indeed from our old Zionist positions. In the old days, since we held that we were not merely a religious but an ethnic group, we argued that our spiritual bond must be not only a cult but a culture. From this, old-time Zionism inferred that Jewish culture had to be made free—in Zion—in order to be sound; and we were inclined to feel that whatever Jewishness might turn into in Zion would be the living Jewish culture. Today we make quite a different inference. Israel is not free to develop culturally as it may please. It is the Zionist duty of Israel to be "Jewish"—that is, to develop in ways appropriate not only to its own situation, but to ours, or perhaps particularly to ours.

However, we must keep in mind the specific function of the view of the Jews as One People united by a common culture: it is supposed to distinguish Zionists *from non-*

Zionists in America. Consequently, just as Diaspora Zionists demand, on the strength of this principle, that Israel must remain "Jewish" so that it can be our spiritual home, so they must logically also demand that Diaspora Jewry qualify itself to share fully in the culture that is to be revived and/or preserved in Israel. The difference between a Zionist and a non-Zionist would then be that non-Zionists did not accept the idea of sharing fully in Israeli culture, and hence would —in the Zionist view—expose us to the danger of ceasing to be One People.

But the idea of sharing a culture rooted in another land and developing in accordance with foreign conditions calls for closer examination. To what extent is it possible? To what extent is it even desirable? What is possible and what is desirable do not constitute absolute principles. If we were to take them as such, we could hardly imagine a real participation in an ethnic culture from abroad. Whatever else an ethnic culture may mean, it means that form of symbolic communication which occurs between all such people as are in effective and continuous social contact and have a common language. Living out of effective social contact with the Israelis, we could do no more than share in an imitation of "ethnic culture" together with them, and that on condition that Hebrew were a living language among us.

But even as to this quasi-ethnic unity, what is possible depends on what is regarded as desirable, and what is desirable—on what is felt to be possible. In Eastern Europe, as we have noted, the Jews (at least, a large proportion of them) thought it both possible and desirable to sustain an ethnic culture of their own in Yiddish, as well as a parallel culture in Hebrew which united them with the Yishuv in Palestine. In order to maintain this situation, they were ready to demand legal guarantees and facilities for Yiddish and Hebrew education. More important even than that, they were prepared for the effort of organization involved in fighting to maintain the Jewish ethnic culture as the primary culture of the Jewish community. No Zionist in America thinks for a moment of proposing this kind of program for us here. We consider ourselves ambitious if we hope to maintain at least a rabbinate and a staff of Hebrew teachers more or less conversant with Hebrew as something between a dead and a foreign language. For the rest we hopefully plan to build "bridges" to Israel by tours, students' visits, by newspaper and magazine reports of events there, and by translations and other forms of cultural exchange.[17]

This, we feel, is about all that is possible; and what we mean is that this much is possible, because only this much—with a distinct straining of the will—is believed to be desirable; and if we are to interpret plainly this last euphemism, what we really mean is that only this much is likely to be tolerated without involving us in too much unpleasantness, under the circumstances of our life in America at this time.

What we sense to be the tolerance level of America at any time depends, of course, on how sensitive we happen to be at the moment. Since the State of Israel was born, there has been a remarkable rise in our sensitivity to the issue of dual loyalties. We ignored the whole matter with calm indifference before then, as we may surmise, for two reasons. First, until the State arose, there was nothing but the devotion of Diaspora Jews (and, above all, its organized expression in the Zionist Movement) to embody our hope for the security and perpetuation of the Jewish People. Now that the State exists, the "common destiny" of the Jewish people depends much less (and certainly not exclusively) upon our Jewish and Zionist loyalty. Hence, we can now "afford" to be sensitive on the issue of loyalty. Secondly, moreover, the loyalty in question was then one to an intangible aspiration, whereas now it means supporting the interests of a tangible, existing sovereign state. This, it would appear, is intrinsically more open to objection than was our devotion to what was then only a hope. Thus, our new definition of Zionism, making Jewish culture primary in it, serves two purposes at once: not only does it relieve us of any responsibility to go to Israel and build it, but it shifts our commitment from a physical entity to a spiritual one. This, we dimly feel, is far less likely to involve us, with non-Jews or non-Zionists, or even in our own minds, in perplexities about the vexed issue of dual loyalties.

But is this really the case? Upon analysis, it is clearly a delusion to suppose that ethnic cultural bonds are intrinsically any less open to suspicion in America than are social and political ones. We can accurately state the factual situation by reversing the proposition: social-political no less than cultural ties to a homeland abroad are an accepted part of the American folkways—but only *up to a certain point*. Both alike are regarded with a degree of suspicion which increases rapidly when it is felt that the point of tolerance has been exceeded.[18] America looks on with an amused indifference or even sympathy when the Irish picket a visiting English dignitary, when Jews hold protest meetings against Britain or the Soviet Union or, for that matter, against the State of Israel, or when Arab representatives attack both the State of Israel and the American Jews. Nobody will imagine that this means there are no circumstances that could make Americans resentful of such attachment to a country abroad. Resentment would certainly arise if some interest upon which the country is strongly united seemed to be threatened. In the same way, America enjoys the colorfulness of folkways and cultural traits brought over from abroad. Yet, under certain circumstances, nothing could more easily arouse hostility in this country than to try to preserve a national culture foreign to this soil. When Germans were regarded as alien enemies in America, their culture too was anathema. The first thing America demands is that "foreigners" learn to think, talk, and act like "natives."

A full scale attempt to "Hebraize" the American Jewish community risks the charge of dual loyalties,[19] no less (if no more) than does a full-blooded, old-style Zionism. dedicated to strengthening the beginnings of Jewish nationality in Israel. Such a program, moreover, involves an effort of a kind and magnitude which are no less tremendous, and which would mean quite as radical a change of mentality as might be needed to achieve a large scale immigration of American Jews to Israel. And we have already indicated that the myth needed to sustain it is far less related to reality than is the myth of the Ingathering of the Exiles.

For the fact is that no variant ethnic culture is possible (or, if you wish, tolerable) in America today. The cultural distinctiveness that *is* possible and tolerable in America, the cloak under which socially segregated groups foster insignificant, picturesque vestiges of their ethnic culture, is the freedom of religious difference alone.

This is a logical conclusion which one can extract from American Zionists only by pushing them relentlessly to the wall. Once pinned down, however, we are forced to admit that Jewish culture, to enable us to continue living permanently as Jews in America, must be Jewish religion. Thus, our American Neo-Zionism implies the demand that Israelis develop a consciously, expressly religious culture, so that we may be one people with them—and so that we may succeed, where otherwise we might fail, in retaining our Jewish identity in America. And our answer to the anti-Zionists turns out to be this: Jews are not really an ethnic group, as we used to say, but essentially a religious brotherhood, as they said; still (and here we differ), we cannot continue to survive unless we are really, effectively one group with Jews everywhere.

Zionists who have considered themselves secular Jews until now find it difficult to accept the full consequences of this trend of thought along which circumstances seem to be driving them. Underlying their hesitancy is one reason, at least, whose seriousness cannot be overlooked. The argument that religion, or any principle of faith and action, must be accepted because it is in harmony with our social and historical "existential" situation goes against the grain, particularly when one has been accustomed to regard his *principles* as establishing the norms to which social, historical, and, above all, personal *conditions* should be made to conform. The secular Zionist thought of himself as under obligations which went counter to social pressures and the drift of personal convenience. His self-respect was based on a feeling of living up to these obligations. He may now face a situation in which some of his obligations are no longer as pressing (the survival of the Jewish people no longer depends as fully on his loyalty); and others, which have become more pressing (the demand to settle in Israel), he is not prepared to perform. Consequently, ideologies suggesting the possibility of a permanent Diaspora existence for the Jewish people are attractive. It is easy to adopt them. But when logic forces the conclusion that such ideologies really mean the acceptance of a religious definition of one's Jewishness, one cannot so easily agree to become religious.

Sociologically considered, religion may, and, to a degree, undoubtedly does, function in the American Jewish community as a symbolic facade giving the odor of conformity as well as of sanctity to our existence. But for an *individual* to live by the ideology which this implies means, first of all, a religious conversion. Those who, like the secular Zionists, had a faith to live by in the past are not likely to overlook the nature of the demand that is implied. They cannot accept a religious ideology without a specific conversion to faith, unless they accept also the loss of self-respect this would entail for people used to living by their beliefs.

There are, of course, many contemporary factors making for a revival of religion, apart from the specific social and historical situation that makes a religious ideology attractive to American Jews. The plight of the world in which we live is certainly critical enough to make anyone consider his "existential" situation at a level far deeper and from a perspective far wider than the relatively superficial sociological conditions of the American Jewish problem. Whoever turns to religion out of such meditations may or may not find his answers in the traditions of Jewish religion. If he does find them there, he will also find a viable ideology for living in the Diaspora under any conditions. Such a solution was available to any Zionist before the State of Israel was founded and remains available today.

But if a Zionist does not—perhaps through experiences quite unrelated to his Zionist dilemma—experience a conversion to religion, then the Neo-Zionist attempt to defend the permanence and normality of the Diaspora leads to two possible alternatives: either to a merely conventional, inauthentic acceptance of Jewish religion, whose sole function is then to hide the reality of Exile from his perception; or to an experience of Exile reduced to nothing more than the Negro's or the alienated Jewish intellectual's plight—an alienhood without cultural significance or justification.

The Difficulties
of the
Religious Solution

ANY RELIGIOUS IDEOLOGY has a great advantage over a secular cult. A religion stands inherently superior to history. It need never justify itself by the probable prediction that its values will be fully realized within the foreseeable future. The religious "myth" is an essentially trans-historical myth; and accordingly its ability to keep high the faith of its "captive audience" is not basically dependent upon the chances of history. For this reason, barring catastrophes, there will, no doubt, always be a traditional Judaism, designed, as it is, to bear the condition of Exile.

But for the very same reason, authentic Jewish traditional religion is relatively independent of the character of a particular time and place. It is under no necessity to be a natural outgrowth of its environment; indeed, in a profound sense it cannot and should not be so. The "natural" condition of "normative" Judaism is the Exile, for Jewish tradition knows only one permanent home, Zion, and that a home to be truly attained in a trans-historical time. The historical effect of the religious concept of Exile has been that Judaism depends on permanency of tenure in *no* home, except ultimately in Zion, so that it can pitch its tent in any place, and abide any ghetto. Thus, too, Jewish tradition can continue unconditionally to live in America, whether in the immigrant ghetto or the invisible ghetto of America-at-large. Knowing that history never makes a final agreement with the Jews (who are not only an eternal people but a people about

[97

whose security of tenure every time and place has its explicit or implicit reservations), traditional Judaism can dwell in America, as anywhere else, prepared for anything history may bring forth, even for the eventuality that this home, too, may become impossible to inhabit, as have so many others.

Nor is traditional Judaism necessarily affected by the success of Zionism in establishing the Jewish State. Zionists among Orthodox Jews may regard this as the beginning of the Messianic era, anti-Zionists as only another pseudo-Messianic episode; but both believe that we still await the ultimate Redemption from Exile, as we did before Israel was founded.

The Question of Exile

Of course, this is *not* the kind of religious ideology which has recently become popular once more in America. Authentic traditional Judaism swims against the stream of the current ideological fashion among American Jews no less than do the cults of secular Jewishness, though perhaps it is able to do so more successfully and longer, because its Messiah is trans-historical. The new religious ideology, however, believes it rides the wave of the future. It needs no exemption from the chances of history, for the natural conditions of American life favor it. It is founded on what seems to many the highly probable myth that Judaism (or rather a naturalized version of it) is truly, integrally at home in America, that it has found here, at long last, a permanent home.

In this respect, the current religious ideology greatly resembles the doctrine of the nineteenth-century Reform movement. That movement, too, was based upon the denial of Exile. The Jews lived in Dispersion, to be sure, but this was precisely their permanent destiny and mission; for this God had chosen them. They were scattered among the Gentiles to be a light unto the nations, bearing witness to the universal truth of monotheism by their devotion to the One God and to His prophetic ethics.

But the new religious ideology cannot adopt the Reform any more than the Orthodox doctrine with a whole heart.

It is unable to accept the Orthodox adjustment to exile, because the new ideology aims at a Judaism naturalized in America, not one prepared to segregate itself, ghetto fashion. It cannot accept the Reform doctrine, because it is unable to swallow the denial of the Exile in this particular form. To deny Exile simply by inverting its meaning so that it becomes a providential Dispersion, as the classic Reform credo did, would involve conceiving the Jews as a Chosen People. This doctrine the new religious ideologists cannot easily accept.[1] As men reared in the Zionist tradition, they are influenced by the criticism of the idea of a Jewish mission to the Gentiles as an apologetic contrivance, with the virtue of neither humility nor self-respect: it is the theory of men vain enough to make the Jews perpetual teachers to the Gentiles, and faint-hearted enough to deny the Jews the right to be themselves without further justification; to be, like any other people, not a means to the true ends of history, but historic ends in themselves.

In the same way, also, the new ideologists feel that the Reform movement dealt unhistorically with the substance of Judaism. They agree that the revelation of God's will to the Jews was not a single, final act completely accomplished at Mount Sinai (not even implicitly complete, as the Orthodox Jews say, making their own bow to the obvious changes in Jewish law throughout history.) They agree with the concept of continuous revelation, as registered through the changes authorized in the tradition by the Jewish social consensus. But if Jewish *history* is the organ through which the revelation to the Jews is registered (just as other revelations may have been vouchsafed through other collective histories), then it follows that certain tests of historic authenticity must be applied. First of all, the newest revelation cannot be a flat rejection of virtually the entire approach and content of the old, but there must be a minimum of organic relationship and continuity. Secondly, the authority which validates the new revelation must be the collective entity through whose history it is revealed: that is, the body Solomon Schechter called Catholic Israel, the people whose life is the substance of Jewish history. Accordingly, any movement which heedlessly abandons major portions of the Jewish tradition, and which, speaking in the name of a small minority, splits the unity of Catholic Israel, forfeits its claim to voice the revelations of the new time.

If this is the test by which the school of Historical or Conservative Judaism (from which most of the new religious ideologists spring) condemns Reform, then one wonders how the abandonment of the concept of Exile by the new ideology can itself escape condemnation. For what can a Jewish community be like, having no idea nor sense of Exile?

There are many great ideas in Judaism: the One God, the Brotherhood of Man, the single, divine source of good *and* evil, the paradoxes of God's foreknowledge and man's freedom, of God's two aspects of Judgment and Mercy, and many, many more. Whether they are uniquely Jewish in their origin or were paralleled in the development of other religious or theosophical systems, these ideas in their combination make Judaism, as we know, one of the great influences and lasting monuments of all human civilization. But we all know, too, that almost everything in Jewish thought can be and has been transplanted, cherished, and made fruitful elsewhere. In the system of Jewish ideas "Exile" is the *inalienably* Jewish idea, the most intimate creation of the Jewish people, the symbol in which our whole historic experience is sublimated and summed up. No other people had the Jewish experience of millennial Exile. All the meaning "Exile" has flows straight from Jewish history, and it gives our history, our being, and our identity as a people its meaning. Live under the sign of Exile—your life as a Jew is an ever-present tension. Cut the idea out—and you cut out memory, identification, and drive, substituting a dull adjustment.

The Jewish world today is full of argument about the Exile. Most of it is vitiated at the source because nobody wishes to remember that Exile is essentially a religious idea.[2] Exile is something God imposed upon the Jews, not Roman Titus. It is a pivot on which the whole cosmic order turns, and not just an expression of the way Gentile society

100]

has treated the Jews in their social, political, and economic relations. Exile is a penance God imposed on the Jewish people for their sins; it is also a cosmic task He set them, for by their holiness in Exile they must bring the Messiah to redeem all the world. One may or may not accept these religious beliefs upon which the meaning of the word "Exile" rests. But these *are* the sources which give the idea meaningfulness; and when we use the word robbed of this meaning we are shooting blank cartridges into the wind. We in America are not in Exile, we say, because nobody keeps us here, nor does anyone keep us out of Israel. The argument is sound—but it is not an argument. The debate is not about exile; it is about "Exile"—Golus, Galut. "Exile" does not depend on the United States Congress nor on the Israeli Knesset. "Exile" means a disordered condition of the Universe as a whole, which is epitomized in the fact and symbol that the Jewish people live outside their own proper place, the land of Israel.

Zionism has had its share in the shrinkage of significance in these terms. But there is a difference between the Old Zionists or the Israelis and the new American Jewish ideology. Their conception of *galut* is a rejection of older concepts; but to reject is to be sharply and actively aware of what one rejects. We here refuse to hear of Exile at all, in any meaning. We thereby renounce our memory.

Jewish history can be divided into cycles dialectically succeeding one another as the implications of the idea of Exile are unfolded. There are Messianic epochs when Exile is passionately rejected, and post-Messianic epochs when Exile is devoutly accepted. The idea of Exile inherently involves a cycle of conflict, and as one or another of its aspects rises uppermost, we have one or another phase of the cycle. That the Children of Israel perfect themselves so that the Exile will be broken and Messiah come—this is the whole purpose of Exile: to come to an end in the cosmic redemption. But the greatest perils lie precisely in the most ardent efforts to bring this about, even though it is God's will. For zeal can become arrogance and the enthusiasm of self-perfection can lead to the delusion that one is perfect, a saint, a prophet, and a redeemer. In its most intense

[101

religious upheavals, Judaism of the Exile gave rise to Sabbatianism, the Frankist movement, and other "pseudo-Messiahs" who announced the supersession of the Law and the onset of the Kingdom of Heaven. Against this Messianism which "forced the end" and prematurely terminated the ordeal of Exile, Jews developed a defense which colored the entire life of Diaspora existence in past centuries. They developed the *cult* of Exile.

There is an expression in Yiddish which conveys the full impact of this cult of the Exile. *"Oprichten golus"*—to *observe* Exile as a rite and a penance.

Exile is a penance, an evil imposed upon Israel—something, therefore, which Israel suffers and is called upon to overcome. Yet the pain and shame of Exile are imposed upon Israel as a signal distinction. It is for this that they are Chosen—for this quite as much as for the Torah and for the Promised Land.

Exile was viewed not simply as a condition visited upon the Jews but as a commitment that they must take upon themselves. It was a vow and a vigil whose aim was still redemption, whose end was still to wipe out Exile and everything it stood for. But to bring this end about was not within man's scope: God in his own good time would grant it. It was for man to take upon himself not only the yoke of the law, but the privations of Exile, and not merely with submission but with an exalted joy.

The Zionist idea was formulated in some aspects by leaders with only tenuous ties to the continuous Jewish tradition. Nevertheless, under any true historical accounting, it linked up directly with the cyclical conversions of the idea of Exile by which the Jewish people sought to know itself. The intellectual substance of Zionism is the rejection of Exile: not the *denial* of Exile, but its rejection. For the Zionist attitude begins with a very lively awareness and affirmation of Exile as a condition. There were two historical attitudes to which Zionism opposed itself, and in opposing, was defined. The first was the acceptance of Exile as a "commitment"—the attitude, by and large, of Orthodox

Jewry at the time. The other was the denial of Exile as a condition—an attitude which arose in Reform Jewry.

Zionism was a movement of revival, an outburst of passion—and its heat came from reaction to what it opposed as false and dead in other movements. Zionism began with the assertion that Exile is a fact—a fact attested by the Dreyfus case—and that its denial by Western Jewries was a base self-delusion. But a Zionism which had nothing more than this to say would have remained sterile. The vitality of Zionism arose from the violence of its opposition to Exile as a cult and Dispersion as a "mission."

The "ideology" of Zionism is almost entirely concerned with demonstrating the existence of Exile as a condition and analyzing its inherent tendencies. How does one demonstrate the existence of Exile and what is meant by an analysis of its trends? All that a secular ideology can possibly concern itself with under these headings are the political, social, and economic complaints of one or another Jewish community in its relations with Gentiles. But is this an idea of sufficient consequence to have fed the memory and imagination of a whole people for so long a time? Clearly not! It is not this idea of exile which gave the Jews matter for ecstasies of thought throughout the centuries. Nor could the determination and analysis of these facts inspire Zionists to political enthusiasm. But Zionism also had a "mystique," a mythology wherein it formed part of the central creative stream of Jewish tradition. The Zionist mystique arises from a passionate rejection of the Jewish "mission" of Reform Judaism, on the one hand, and of Orthodox Judaism's cult of Exile, on the other. In both Zionism saw empty words, "conventional lies" masking a weak surrender. Western Jewry surrendered to Gentile culture and Eastern Jewry to Gentile social oppression. Both used high-flown phrases that had lost all meaning. They spoke of "missions" and of "penances," implying a heroic commitment in the old style, but in fact, what in the East pretended to be exalted submission was supine defensiveness and what in the West pretended to be high-minded devotion was just smug rhetoric. Against both Zionism proposed its own culture of Biblical heroism. It proposed again to bring the motif of Redemption into the picture of contemporary Jewish history.

And now we have ourselves, the American Jews after the establishment of the State of Israel. We don't think we are in Exile. Well, why should we? The idea of Exile is no longer a basic category of our thought—better, perhaps, (one should say with Kant) of our perception—about which there can be no question. *It has become debatable*—Zionism for one, has made it so. If Exile has become an item in an ideology, it should be a clear and distinct idea, not a protean, archetypical figure of speech. Are we, strictly speaking, in a condition of political and social exile? Obviously not. The most that can be clearly proved is that we still have some Jewish problems. Even whether we have *the* Jewish Problem is controversial. That we suffer from "abnormality" is not beyond question.

It is much easier to feel that the cosmos is disordered, that God's *Shekhinah* is in Exile, than that we are. It was because of us, once, that God banished His own Presence to the Exile—so we are instructed. But though we can very easily believe in Exile of the *Shekhinah,* we cannot find any way to believe in our own. We find it hard to suppose that the original disordering of the cosmos was at all related to our banishment—and if the poor *Shekhinah* had to wait upon American Jewry's yearning for redemption, she could at once give up all hope of the Messiah.

Nevertheless—we persist; we survive as Jews. We have lost the memory of who we are and the sense of why we are—and yet we exist. What other hope can we have than that out of this strange Limbo in which we reside will come to us a new sense of Exile that will give purpose and direction to our life?

The Question
of Definition

The new religious ideology, however, has lost the sense of Exile. Rather, to put the Exile out of our minds is its primary purpose. Indeed, the protagonists of the new theory become quite impatient when anyone tries to remind them of the Exile. Thus, Dr. Jacob B. Agus says, *"Those who have no faith in America obviously cannot be trusted with the task of building the future of Jewry in America."*[3] He practically suggests that such persons be excommunicated. "(The community) need repudiate only such groups as negate the value of our continued existence in the Diaspora —whether in the name of a totalitarian Zionism or in the name of totalitarian Americanism."[4]

But when it comes to the question whom the community should *include,* the religious ideology encounters a new difficulty—a difficulty of definition. Definition, moreover, becomes a serious problem in regard not only to, Who is a Jew? but to, What is Judaism? Both these questions had easy and natural answers (hence they did not really arise) so long as the sense of Exile had not been deadened. Everyone was a Jew who shared the Jewish Exile; and Judaism was the historic experience of that whole people, as it found expression in the religious culture that summed up our many-faceted fate of Exile. With the sense of Exile dulled and with religious belief substituted as the criterion of Jewishness, grave questions arise as to both definitions. There is the implicit demand that a Jew prove himself by belief, and that any tenet or practice of Judaism prove itself worthy to be believed, especially by a modern Jew fully integrated in twentieth-century America.

It is fairly well agreed that, even though the Jewish community may be most easily accepted in America as a religious entity, and though the inclination to accept this title is growing among Jews themselves, it remains seriously in doubt what part of American Jews are actually "religious"—or what, indeed, is the meaning of "religion" as applied to them. This view is expressed quite emphatically by one of the most prominent ideologists of naturalized American Jewish religion. Dr. Mordecai M. Kaplan says, "Jews at present resemble a demobilized army ... With the decay of supernaturalistic religion as a uniting bond, no other cohesive force has thus far been generated. Jewish unity, whatever of it still exists, is buttressed from *without* by the Christian tradition and by its offspring anti-Semitism, but its *inner* supports are crumbling."[5] In order to escape from their "spiritual isolation and moral anomie," Jews "desperately" build synagogues and religious schools. They face "inevitable frustrations" in their flight to religion, because "though their spiritual leaders have long abandoned supernaturalism they have not replaced it with any other dedicated faith." As for the schools, 'the number of men and women ... *qualified* to teach Jewish subject matter is shockingly small," and so low do American parents rate the degree of Jewish culture they need to transmit to their children that attendance is low, brief, and perfunctory: "The Jewish religious schools are like the subway trains always full, with people constantly getting on and getting off at every station."[6] What wonder then that the most gifted spirits among American Jews cannot "be associated with any type or normative Judaism," that few "of our bright young Jews are really interested in Judaism or Jewish culture," and that even among the "synagogued" Jews there are few who really live the Judaism that they "profess to believe in."[7] In other words, Dr. Kaplan is not content with having so many Jews come to roost under the wing of the synagogue, for what he earnestly wishes is that he could feel them to be real Jews.

If one feels that we are dealing no longer with real Jews but with Jews who still have to be converted into the real thing, then of course, questions of definition become serious questions. Dr. Kaplan's view on this point is well known. He has always felt that one could almost reduce the entire contemporary Jewish Problem to one cardinal difficulty: We have lost a defined status as a community.[8] Agus realizes that "the most telling objection against the conception of a religious status for American Jewry is the indubitable fact of its limited inclusiveness." He suggests that one could adopt "two complementary definitions" demarcating "nuclear and protoplasmic sections" of Jewry, the former consisting of strict observers, the latter distinguished from Gentiles only by the "inexorable hairline of conversion." Still, this would leave in the outer darkness of the protoplasmic section "many spiritually sensitive people unaffiliated with the synagogue, yet ... profoundly stirred by Jewish associations"; and it would include in the inner circle of the nucleus "masses of indifferent materialists . . . cold and unmoved by an appeal to spiritual values."[9] Nonetheless, when facts fail to accord with the definition, all Dr. Agus can suggest is that we are obliged to bring them into conformity: so seriously does he take the definition!

This is a difficulty that never really bothered the Orthodox Jews, the Yiddishists and ethnic autonomists, and the old-line Zionists, for all of these never doubted that they constituted groups of real Jews. As a result, whatever the disapproval and outright hostility which each may have felt to the others at times, or in general to other kinds of Jews outside their own party, they never viewed them with that peculiar troubled irritability of the religious ideologists towards Jews who escape their definitions; they never doubted the validity of other Jews' credentials or the reality behind their own! There was an underlying sense of easy brotherhood towards all Jews, precisely because it was so obvious the Jews were a real thing. The Orthodox knew beyond question that all the seed of Abraham were included in the Covenant, and if they rebelled against God, they were simply bad Jews—*poshei Yisrael*—but as real as any other. The Yiddishists and ethnic autonomists were, perhaps, somewhat limited in their Jewish perception, effectively feeling as their fellow Jews mainly the Yiddish-speaking community, but though the historic bond that bound them to Sefardim or to the "assimilated" Jews of the West may have thinned, it was of such a kind that by extension it could include them, too: if *history* made one a Jew, all who shared it were indubitably real Jews. We, the Zionists, felt most keenly the critical and problematic state of Jewish existence. We arose out of a sense of the disintegration and collapse of the Jewish people. But by our very rise, by our assertion and drive toward a common destiny, we overcame the problem in the moment of grasping it, we gave body to the Jewish people in the moment of evoking its national will—and in that moment, too, we (together with the Yiddishists) gave freedom and creative élan to Jewish culture.

This, also, is a source of great perplexity to the new religious ideologists, as it is not only "Jew" but "Judaism" which appears to them to be seriously in need of redefinition. For they are afflicted, here too, by severe doubts that what really exists as Jewish religious culture is valid, and they are driven to anxious efforts in order to conjure into reality that which by their definition Judaism ideally is. I need not quote from Dr. Kaplan, since it is well known that his whole life has been given over to the passion of reconstructing Juadism in order to shape it into something that will fit his definition of a contemporary this-worldly "salvational" system.

Dr. Agus is in the so-called right wing of American Conservative Judaism, yet he, too, is unable to accept Jewish tradition simply as it has been handed down to us by what Solomon Schechter called Catholic Israel, namely, the consensus of generations upon generations of pious Jews. While accepting the law as given—at least to start with—Dr. Agus refuses to accept the methods of reasoning through which the rabbis formerly derived the laws. He is very actively concerned with *rethinking* the body of law, just as is Dr. Kaplan, and he applies the same methods of thought as Dr. Kaplan, namely, the universal logic of all men and not the traditional logic of the Talmud. What differs is that the aim he ultimately accepts is not "this-worldly" like Dr. Kaplan's, but (superficially, at least) "other-worldly." To be recognized by him as valid for Judaism today, any traditional practice (or proposed departure from it) must be shown to conduce toward making contemporary American Jews more pious.[10] In this revision of Jewish religious culture, presumably, Dr. Agus sees the contemporary phase of progressive revelation in history.

Now, obviously, the whole Jewish people, the collective subject of Jewish history, does not live for the sake of making technical decisions on what changes in ritual would inspire greater piety among the synagogue members of contemporary America, given their temperaments, distractions, level of knowledge and commitment and other circumstances. Not the historic Jewish people, but a small committee of rabbis in the Conservative movement is conceived of as the organ for this revelation. That there must be some such contraction of Solomon Schechter's original (undoubtedly rather vague) idea of Catholic Israel is recognized quite explicitly by Robert Gordis: "... Catholic Israel must be conceived of differently from hitherto accepted views ... Catholic Israel embraces all those who observe Jewish law in general, although they may violate one or another segment of it, and who are sensitive to the problem of their non-observance because they wish to respect the authority of Jewish law."[11] Dr. Gordis wishes to include under the title "Catholic Israel" a vague group not confined to a particular Jewish denomination. But whom, in fact, does this definition suit more perfectly than the adherents of Conservative Judaism in America—or, even more specifically, of the "group mind" emerging out of the collective cogitations of the Law Committee of the Conservative Rabbinical Assembly? It is to this that Catholic Israel has shrunk. And the idea of Catholic Israel, so defined, has only one function: the function of reducing the traditional religious culture of Judaism to the dimensions of a contemporary American cult.

Such a theory may certainly be in harmony with the sociological trends in American Jewry. It can serve very well as an ideology for a generation of Jews who have concluded that they *do* want to be Jews and, in any case, are going to have to be Jews, and who would like to feel as much at ease as possible in their Judaism. At the same time one cannot overlook how self-contradictory such a theory is logically—and how self-defeating religiously. For of what religious or logical significance can the test be which proves one is a real Jew, according to the authentic, historically revealed faith and practice of Judaism, when one has previously in committee readjusted Judaism precisely in such a way that the average Jew will find it easy to believe and convenient to practice?

The absurdity of the position is not totally unknown to the new ideologists. From time to time, Mordecai Kaplan shows a clear understanding that history must be taken much more seriously than this if it is to be proposed as an organ of progressive revelation. Catholic Israel can only create new religious insights through history if it is a body capable of having a history.

What Dr. Kaplan's view is emerges quite clearly from the kind of demands he makes upon the secular Zionists in Israel and upon the World Zionist movement, as well as from the proposals he makes for the reconstruction of the American Jewish community. Israel must help save American Jews, according to Kaplan, by not only living a full ethical, Jewishly inspired life-in-this-world, but also formulating its practices as principles and expressing these as ceremonies which could be adopted by the Jewish cult in America: in other words, he asks the Israelis to create that *culture* that could give body and substance and vitality to Judaism as a *cult*. The same tendency is apparent in Dr. Kaplan's proposals for an "organic" Jewish community in America. He cannot be satisfied with a synagogue Judaism alone, even though (since Jewishness must be defined mainly as a cult in America) he defends the centrality of the synagogue. But, clustered around the synagogue, he demands that there be maintained in organic relationship—that is to say, in some sort of organized, democratically responsible unity—a whole array of "legislative" and administrative, social, economic, educational, welfare and "civic defense" activities. In other words, he wishes to give even American Jewry, as far as possible, the scope of a people, not of a union of congregations, and Judaism in America the aspect of a culture, not only a cult. Only in this way can there be a Catholic Israel in any significant sense.

The Meaning of Catholic Israel

Under any definition of what constitutes Catholic Israel, the idea involves certain consequences which its exponents obviously have hidden from themselves. It implies, first of all, a special Jewish "social consensus" separate and different from the general American consensus, but in some sense necessarily identical with the consensus of the Jews as a global people. It involves, consequently, an implicit concession that Jewish culture cannot ever be wholly naturalized in America, nor can the Jewish people lose the uniqueness of a people exclusively identified with a world religion. It means, finally, an implicit assumption that the Jews are, in some sense at least, a Chosen People.

Like many terms essential to an understanding of the Jewish Problem, the idea of a Chosen People is a religious concept undergoing secular transformation because of its historic effects. This may be noted not only in Jewish but in general history. There is a sense in which it may be said that the American people, for example, is a Chosen People. That this is a tenable claim, the Americans, who speak of their land as God's Own Country, show every evidence of believing.

Why is it that Americans lay so much stress on the fact that they are *different*? To be anything at all, you have to be different. If there is such a thing as an American, it must be something different, let us say, from a Frenchman or an Englishman. But some people—the "Chosen Peoples"—can boast that they are different in a way that sets them apart from and above others. Every people celebrates its history in its own calendar, and the heroes and sanctities it memorializes establish a common series of patterns by which each succeeding generation of the people, in its own way, shapes its special character. Not in every folk calendar, however, are the men and events idealized so significant that world history as well as national history is felt to be molded in their image. Only the Chosen Peoples can think the whole of history depends on the major events in their own history.

It is generally the old and fully formed, as well as larger, nations that see world history from the vantage points of their own calendar. For the Italians world history has two turning points, Ancient Rome and the Renaissance; for the Germans, Luther is the great fork in the history of the world, for the French, the Revolution—and so on. America, from its very beginning, when it had far less claim than it has today to national individuality, already regarded its own history as altering the whole character of world history. With America a new chapter begins. Two dates in our national calendar are points of observation from which (we feel) all mankind looked down on new vistas:

Columbus Day and the Fourth of July. We are the New World, the frontier, the land of opportunity, the melting pot in which all the problems of the Old World are cancelled, the laboratory from which has come a new, an American way of life which in this, the American Century, has a mission to reproduce itself throughout the world.

We say that Americans are different with a sort of pugnacious pride. When we say Jews are different, it is either with irritation ("Why do Jews persist in being different?") or with a certain defiance that almost despairs of being understood. Yet it is important, if we wish to understand the Jewish Question, or any particular Jewish question for that matter, to realize that Jews *are* different, and to see just how and why that is so.

There should be nothing strange in saying that the Jews, too, are a Chosen People. They were, of course (and, from the Jewish viewpoint, still remain), *the* Chosen People, in the exact and specific connotation of that title: chosen by God to receive the Revelation of His Word and to live by it in the sight of all mankind. But we have been using the words "a Chosen People" in a derived sense, so that we could say, for example, that the Americans are a "Chosen People."

In this sense the Jews "too"—like the British, French and Germans—are a chosen people. They "too" consider world history as essentially and integrally related to their own. They regard the traumatically memorable occasions in their own history as the hinges on which all of world history swings. Not only pious Jews but, at bottom, all Jews date the real beginning of world history from the Revelation at Mount Sinai, and they cannot help feeling that the Jewish Exile represents a historic breaking point, just as the Messianic era, which is associated in Jewish tradition with our own Restoration to Zion, will signify the ultimate reparation of the world.

For a true comprehension of what it is to be a Jew, one should try to grasp the strangeness, the boldness, the unheard-of, cool, profound self-assurance of the Jews' assuming, as a matter of course, as a first premise that needs no arguing and hardly deserves to be mentioned, that all of world history revolves around their own history. Remember that it is another Jewish intuition—and a profoundly true one—that Jews have really had no history, in the ordinary sense, at least, since the Exile. The Jews were quite conscious how much they differed from the Gentiles in this respect. If the Jews boasted that their existence did not depend on natural causes—"Israel is not subject to the conjunctions of the planets"—it was only an inverted expression of their constant awareness that only miracles could keep them alive. Their role in history was only to suffer the oppression of the four successive Gentile realms whose chronicles made up actual history ever since the Jewish Exile; and no historic action of theirs, not even their piety, but only the miracle of God's mercy, kept them alive through it all. What is known as world history, then, is entirely an affair of the Gentiles.

Yet the deepest Jewish belief remains that the real history of the world is, after all, the history the Jews as a people have known. What happens among the Gentiles during the period the Jews are in Exile is essentially irrelevant—or it is relevant only in so far as it bears upon the purgation of the Jews. This is astonishing enough. But even more astonishing is the fact that the Gentiles, the nations who are every day making actual history, upon whom the fate of the Jewish Diaspora entirely depends, who every day decide it again for good or for ill, they, too, agree in very great measure with the Jewish view of history, and of the Jewish place in it. There are differences, of course: the Gentiles feel that it is Jewish suffering which is essentially irrelevant and non-historical, for it is the Church which is now the hero of the drama of Salvation, and Jews persist only because their Exile is necessary as testimony to the Church's truth and their own error. Yet the Gentile view, too, is that the essential history of the world turns upon Jewish history; that since the advent of Christ, with which is coupled the Jewish Exile and spiritual dispossession, history has passed its last critical point and is now essentially meaningless except as a long purgation looking towards the second, conclusive advent of the Messiah. And at that point the Jews too are to play a central role in the closing act of history—redeemed, however, by renouncing at last their error.

It is clear (speaking now in terms of a secular historical analysis) that one of the reasons Jews were able to persist among the Gentiles is this remarkable accord of their historical conceptions. That Jews had a role to play in the Christian drama of divine history is undoubtedly one of the reasons why they were not utterly destroyed by the Gentiles. We should not underestimate the difficulties of the restraint this involved. For Jewish world history and Gentile world history may indeed have been two faces of the same coin. But if so, it was a coin one of whose faces bore values in a relation directly negative to those inscribed on the other face.

If, then, we mean by a chosen people one that regards its own national history as crucial to world history, the Jews have always been even in this sense a chosen people. Their right to have their national history so regarded is certainly as universally recognized as is the right of the British, French, Germans or Italians. But unlike all other peoples whose national histories are crucial to the history of the world, the Jews' very right to be called *a nation,* and hence to have national history of their own, is (and for two thousand years has been) far from clear. The Jews, until recently, have not been an independent, sovereign entity capable of creating its own history. Yet they not only survived through two thousand years of subjection and dispersion—in itself an historical puzzle—but all that time persisted in regarding what happened to them as the essential frame of reference for whatever happened in history.

The implications of this become even more striking if we consider the matter from another angle. What the Jews did was, as a subject people, to maintain a "social consensus" totally distinct from that of the peoples among whom they lived.

The idea of a unitary consensus of ideas and attitudes underlying social cohesion is one of the most popular ideas

114]

among social scientists today. It is one of the essentials they consider prerequisite to the mysterious quality of societies which they call "integration." It is well understood in contemporary social theory that an "integrated" social group is made up of "differentiated," or conflicting elements, who are nevertheless so related to each other through the "interdependence" of their acts that they continuously appear as a collective unit in the face of the outside world. But (though this subject has been less thoroughly explored) social scientists seem to feel rather differently on the subject of the social consensus. An "integrated" society, they assume, cannot be composed of elements holding radically "differentiated" basic attitudes, but it requires as its foundation a *single* consensus of ideas and attitudes. For if a society held within it several such consensuses, however closely related, it would really not be one but several societies ... Yet in the case of the Jews, at least, we have a group which long lived as part of societies with which it did *not* share a consensus of ideas and attitudes, but maintained its own specific consensus.

On closer examination it is clear, of course, that even the unitary consensus that a territorial nation is supposed to possess must necessarily be a heterogeneous, composite kind of affair. One can discriminate at least two different components of such a consensus. There is, first of all, the component of formally established national institutions such as law, to choose the most obvious example. Institutions of this kind, forming the basis of "legitimacy" in a particular national community, have usually been formulated by an intellectual elite in the nation—lawyers, legislators, political philosophers, and so on—and are more or less automatically acceded to by the mass of the people. If culture is termed "mythological," the closer it is to the life of the masses and "ideological" the more it is directly formed by the intellectual elite, then the ideas and attitudes expressed in these formal institutions to a great extent are ideological.[12] Nevertheless, they enter into the social consensus—that is, they are ideas and attitudes which all the people share—for two reasons: first, because in part they embody elements of the customs, folkways and national mythology in which the whole people shares, and which is implied in the national history; second, because even though another part is derived by certain formal procedures that only the intellectuals really understand, the whole people agrees in accepting the results arrived at as legitimate and authoritative. Thus, while it is certain that such a national institution as the law enters into the social consensus of every nation, the methods and many findings of legal debate are not part of the culture shared by the entire people. Lawyers, legislators, and political philosophers can often have the most violent ideological disputes without any particular effect on the national consensus, which is not really involved at this level. When ideological differences do involve the whole people, the consensus to this extent breaks down and a revolutionary change in the national institutions may be attempted.

A second component of the social consensus is represented by what we might call the informal "institutions" of the nation, its folkways and *mores,* its style and values, and its national myth. The best example (if by "best" we mean "extreme") of such an informal institution is a national language. Nothing can be more certain than that the national language is an indispensable part of the consensus that holds an "integrated" nation together. But at the same time it is obviously beside the point to talk of the people's "consenting" to the language or accepting it as "legitimate" and binding upon them. The language is institutionalized in any society in a way quite different from the formal institutions which the people "accedes to." It is shared quite involuntarily—as is the whole "mythological" realm of an ethnic culture—for it enters into the social consensus by gaining general acceptance not through the popular will but through the popular feeling. A particular phrase, anecdote, myth, game, ritual or fashion which acquires currency or even attains a permanent place in popular or mythic culture—that is, becomes part of the informal (or better, the substantive) institutions of a group—is not accepted because accredited intellectuals through accepted procedures have produced it, and hence it is formally legitimate. It wins its way through its own inherent appeal, through its charm, in fact, of which every man is a qualified judge, or more accurately, an eligible victim. Such an idea or attitude enters into the social consensus when the people as a whole "accepts" it not because it is right and legitimate in its form, but because it is right and attractive in substance.

Now it is clear enough that this part of the social consensus—the "informal" institutions of a society—hardly lends itself to relatively clean-cut definition, as do the formal institutions. How uniformly and unequivocally any substantive cultural value enjoys "acceptance" by the people is a very difficult thing to determine, as even such a basic element of the consensus as the language itself illustrates. Words, idioms, terms of expression vary widely in their universality and usage, and we know well enough how readily whole dialects and special lingoes, not to speak of fashions in slang, rise and subside within a national language, Other elements of the "mythological" realm of culture vary even more widely, and sometimes with a particular bearing upon the problem of maintaining the "integration" of the society through its social consensus. Agreement in terms of language and myth is far more fundamentally essential to social life than is acceptance of authoritative ideas, for while we can imagine groups without an elaborate ideology, we cannot imagine them without a common means of communication and understanding, a common store of words and images, gestures and allusions, expressions wherein much more is implicitly understood than expressly stated. Yet, at the same time, myth is precisely that part of culture in which the greatest leeway can be given for the most personal, the most eccentric, even the most rebellious expressions of sentiment: precisely, perhaps, because more can be implied than is expressly stated. The cultural myth remains closest to the personal experience, just as its substance makes the most direct appeal to the common understanding. Hence myth may express rebellion against the status quo in a variety of forms, which, however, usually remain innocuous—through humor, through symbolic sublimation, and so on. The practical effect of these "rebellious" expressions may be precisely to teach how life under oppression may be borne with dignity, or even with *joie de vivre*.

Thus, both the ideological and the mythic components of a developed social consensus represent a sort of precipitate, a deposit of cultural matter upon which the whole of a society agrees, out of a larger quantity of both ideological and mythic materials which exists, so to speak, in solution and upon which the widest differences of attitude or opinion may exist. There can be ideological differences among intellectuals by which the mass of society is not in the least affected; and the group mythology allows for a wide range of individual and collective variations and innovations without effect upon the social consensus. Now, we can follow our chemical analogy even farther, for we have already noted in passing what is the process through which the social consensus is precipitated out of the cultural solution: An ideological element cannot impose itself upon the mythic materials of mass culture—which means to appeal for validity not merely on formal but on substantive grounds—without claiming to enter into the social consensus. On the other hand, any variation on a mythic theme which is taken up by the intellectuals and ideologized—which means to appeal not merely to popular feeling but to popular will, and to claim validity not merely as a substantively attractive image, but as a logically necessary idea—thereby also claims to enter the social consensus. The chemical structure of the consensus is the compound of myth and ideology, the union of seduction and legitimacy.

An "integrated" society, then, is expected to have one and only one social consensus, one and only one "legitimate" set of ideas and attitudes crystallized out of the popular myth and formulated by the ideological elite. In addition, it usually has a fringe of academic ideological differences not carried down into the substance of myth, and popular mythic variations not set up as necessary ideas. But if such myths and ideologies unite and interpenetrate in a new form, establishing a new consensus, it constitutes (according to the ideas implicit in contemporary social science) a threat to overthrow or dismember the society— and it has usually been treated as such in the actual practice of historic societies.

Consider then what the Jews have represented for two thousand years in Gentile society! How different it is from the relations between other "differentiated" elements in the "integrated" total group! Think, for example, of the moral consensus between master and slave, lord and serf in pre-capitalist society, or of ruler and ruled today. Though too much can easily be made of the idea, there is obviously much truth in the observation that a common ethos was shared by master and slave, lord and serf, assigning the proper place and attitude which each must assume toward the other. The breakdown of traditionalist society has not eliminated in the modern nation the acceptance by both superior and inferior, masses and elite, majority and minority, of a common scale of values, predominantly organized from the perspective of the rulers. Within this scale of values, to be sure, certain ambiguities are introduced continually through the resentments of the underdog. These "counter-mores," these polarities of attitude and opposed feelings (like the complementary colors in impressionist painting which only give body to the basic tones of which they serve as the shadows) crop up usually in myth, not in ideology. They do not challenge the existing hierarchy of values; they merely outline the strain of its suspension over the brute facts of rule and resentment. Among the elite, for their part, we are likely to find heresies of a more or less academic character; and if some independent ideologist applies his "free-floating" intelligence to a social problem, he often produces a pale Utopia, with no passion behind it. But when, indeed, the intellectual unites himself to the resentful mass and transfuses their myth into his ideology, or when the mass hardens its mythic ironies into ideological certainties, this is usually the signal of revolution and disintegrative change.

The Jews certainly have never had the least impulse, nor the least chance, to revolutionize the societies in which they lived. In the very early days of their millennial Exile, they adopted the principle that "The laws of the authorities are legitimate," and implicit in their entire national myth was the acceptance of social subjection, of submission to the Gentiles until Messiah came. Yet at the same time the Jews have been able to maintain—and usually with the consent of their rulers!—not a mere mythological dissidence, nor a merely academic ideological dissent, but a full-fledged independent social consensus of their own, the mythic-ideological independence of a Chosen People.

The Jews, wherever they lived, had a traditional set of values, which was both formally and substantively independent of Gentile culture. Their historic time reckoning was their own, and it stood its ground in sturdy independence alongside the year count of the Christians and the Moslems, and later of the French and Russian and Fascist Revolutions. Their sacred calendar of festivals and fast days was their own, marking out a different rhythm from the saint-days of the Christians. Their historic coordinates to which to refer all events were the Revelation at Mount Sinai and the future Return to Zion, rather than Calvary or the Hegira, or the Italian Renaissance, the Lutheran Reformation, the British Glorious Rebellion, the American, French or Russian Revolutions. They had their own distinct mythic space orientations. They faced towards Jerusalem to pray, and, with Judah Halevi, they regarded the Land of Israel, not Rome or Greenwich, as the earth's heart and reference point.

The distinctive culture of the Jews was not the innocent myth of a provincial tribe, the colorful folkways of some autochthonous peasant stock that add variety to a national culture. Even in their own country—and how much the more when they became dispersed through the globe—Jewish culture was a self-conscious bearer of values claiming universal and ultimate significance. It was from first to last a culture which stood as a solid integrated block, because in it the intellectual and the popular mind were interpenetrated and merged.

How extraordinary, how decisive even, has been the role of the intellectual in the Jewish community! To what an unparalleled degree has he formed the religious culture and moral civilization of the Jews at their lower as well as higher levels! He gave them not only ideology but *mythos,* not only form but matter, not only an order but much of the substance of values. The Jewish rituals of purity, long since common to the whole congregation of believing

Israel, still bear the marks of their origin among priests and Pharisees.[13] Through the deliberate design of intellectuals, we Jews became for centuries a people of priests. It is characteristic of the traditional Jewish intellectuals, of the rabbis and teachers, that they defined the sphere of their activity as Law, posing in this way a demand for the reception by the people of their special attitudes. But their Law, though it was derived and codified by a class of specialists distinct from the laity and with elaborate formal methods of analysis —the seven, thirteen, or, according to one authority, 613 modes of interpretation—their Law was far from restricting itself either in subject matter or in method to technical limits. It was only because of their broad range and flexible approach, approximating the manner of thought of the people themselves, that Jewish intellectuals could have such an influence. The Law, even in the form of *halakhah*—practice—covered creed, ritual, ethics, etiquette, no less than civic legislation. In the form of *agadah*—preaching—it invaded every realm of poetry and myth. By an unprecedented effort of mass education, persisted in over centuries, the myth-making imagination of the Jewish people, suffused with the poetry of *agadah* and the power of *halakhah,* became closely wedded to an ideological, literary tradition.

The Jewish community was a constitutionally ruled society and its constitution was Jewish literature. The sway of the Torah extended among the Jews into a far wider range of behavior and influenced the motives of conduct far more deeply than any other constitutional law has ever done, even including the Koran. It was not the rule of courts alone, but it sought to determine the minutest etiquette of the people. It was first of all an affirmative influence, a seed bed for fertile imaginations. The Law was not only feared and studied; it entered into the myth making of the common people, and its traditions were worked into their poetry. The Law embodied mysticism, scientific imagination, humor, grief; the whole lifeblood of the people remained within it. But the Law, or its literary tradition, was also a negative, a regulative influence on Jewish self-expression. It proposed on occasion to control every phase of self-expression, down to the slightest gestures, under the idea of Israel's special relation to God. The Bible warns the Jews against "walking in the ways of the nations," meaning specifically the seven heathen nations of Canaan, but this maxim was applied by Jews to all the folkways of the Gentiles. It is well known how many arts and folkways of the Gentiles—such as painting and athletic sports—were frowned on by the normative Jewish tradition, and how whole realms of literature, science and general culture were prone to be deliberately neglected if it was feared that they clashed with the spirit and letters of Israel. What was picked up out of general folkways—musical modes, foreign languages and even styles of costume—could on the other hand acquire such sanction under the aegis of tradition that piety preserved it in new times and new circumstances. Thus the whole range of custom, fashion, and informal expression could be called to pass muster before the critical eye of the tradition and its criteria of taste. Everything in Jewish traditional culture (and it recorded and preserved the age-old experience of a world-people) was pressed into a harmony, specifically different from that of the host Gentiles and founded on the Scriptures, precedents, and the fourfold traditional logic of a universal religion. Nothing like it has ever been seen.

The Jews, then, most markedly in Eastern Europe but quite plainly everywhere else they lived among Gentiles until their Emancipation, maintained a distinct and separate social consensus of their own. Their interpenetrated mythic and ideological culture presented a solid structure of independent legitimacy which was neither subordinate to the ideas of their rulers nor even organically related to the particular times and places where they lived. Thus they lived in history as above history, in a social framework as apart from it, and in a spatial context as distinct from it. Exile was for them a wall—at times a thick wall, and at other times a flimsy membrane—to shelter their independence of the environment upon which they depended. Within this alienation of the group, they were whole as individuals, in spite of the unprecedented, the veritably abnormal state of their being. The Gentiles, too, recognized the unique Jewish position, for in the lay consensus of Christian society the Jew was recognized as the alien whose right of domicile never made him a brother; and in their religious consensus the Jew was imaged as that ultimate infidel who would persist among them unconverted till the Second Advent.

It is not difficult to perceive why the Jews were able to maintain so remarkable a distinction. The basis of their special social consensus was their religion. Not only Judaism but all religions provide for their believers a consensus not bound to place or time and distinct from the special social consensus of the nation. But among all other peoples, the consensus of religion crosses the lines of nationality to unite believers of many different ethnic affiliations in a single communion. Among Jews alone religion serves to single out and reinforce the membership of a unique ethnic communion.

Any appeal to the tribunal of Catholic Israel, indeed any attempt to establish Jewishness upon the criterion of Jewish religious belief, leads ultimately to the same effect. It may strive to naturalize the Jewish community in a given time and place, but however superficial it may try to make its Jewish individuality, it implies a commitment with potentially profound consequences. For it reinforces the very principle through which Israel becomes Catholic Israel and the Jewish people a Chosen People. The very crux of the strange Exile in which the Jewish spirit is today plunged is that this consequence is not only unknown but unwanted. It is not a destiny that the modern Diaspora Jew gladly assumes, but a fate from which he tries to hide himself. Foremost among those who try to obscure the true situation are those very religious ideologists whose efforts, in the long run, may contribute most effectively toward maintaining it.

A Zionist View
of the Contemporary
Situation

IN OUR WHOLE DISCUSSION
to this point, there has been a certain distortion of perspective because we assumed the centrality of the American
Jewish situation and problem. Even from this point of departure, it was evident that the American Jewish problem is
intimately involved with the global Jewish problem. But if
we take a global point of view, then not America but Israel
is central in the contemporary Jewish situation. Jewish
history will certainly describe the present period as primarily the epoch of the Ingathering of the Exiles. For a proper
understanding of the American Jewish problem, it is essential to analyze the American situation, too, as it relates to
the Ingathering of the Exiles.

So overwhelming were the changes in the Jewish situation caused by Nazism, the Second World War, and the swift
Jewish victory by which the State of Israel was established
that we rarely consider the radical transformation that has
been going on every year since then. For seven years we have
seen the Jewish community of one country after another
removed from Exile and resettled practically intact in Israel.
The refugees in the German DP camps or the broken communities of such countries as Bulgaria and Yugoslavia came
to Israel *en masse*. Virtually all Jews in a number of Arab
countries—notably Iraq and Yemen—ended their Exile and
settled in a body in Israel. The Jewish communities today
remaining in Eastern Europe and in Moslem countries face
the question of mass emigration to Israel as a matter of

immediate urgency. In some places, obstacles prevent a large-scale exodus—notably in the Soviet Union and its satellites, and also, in different ways, in Egypt and North Africa. But the alternative to exodus in those countries is a future in which the possibility of maintaining a Jewish community under tolerable conditions, or sometimes of maintaining it at all, has become dubious.

A man who returned from Israel to Austria, in order to reclaim property or take up an old profession, or for whatever reason, knew clearly that he was abandoning a living Jewish community for a land in which no real Jewish community did or could, or even should, any longer exist. He, together with other aging and Jewishly impotent survivors, would live out their lives isolated from the Jewish people. Hardly different is the plight of Jews behind the Iron Curtain. Those who succeeded in leaving and going to Israel will live on as Jews. Of the others, only the religious Jews may be able to preserve a meager reminder of the community that once flourished. It is clear that no secular Jewish culture or community will grow in the Jewish wastes of Russia or Poland. In North Africa, too, those Jews who succeed in settling in Israel feel they are taking up a new, free, secure Jewish life, while those remaining behind know that they may easily face a situation of neither freedom nor security. There is a sifting going on in the Jewish world. Broken Jewish communities, or Jewish communities still breaking up, are dividing, as in a centrifuge, into a stream moving to Israel to combine as a new community and immobile individuals who stay behind, to face a Jewish future that has become acutely questionable.

The force of this attraction to Israel is felt even in countries where the future of the Jewish community still seems relatively secure, including those where (using the terms of our previous analysis) the Jewish emancipation was established without crisis. Naturally enough, the response is most evident in countries like England, where an appreciable general tendency to emigrate exists; or in countries like South Africa and Argentina, where general social and political instability recall to Jewish folk wisdom the situation of other Exiles, in which Jews became the scapegoats of social upheaval. Equally naturally, there is little response in a stable and expanding country like the United States, where no general tendency to emigrate exists; though, of course, a small, steady stream of young Jews continues (at about the same rate as twenty years ago) to go to settle in Israel. Yet this does not mean that American Jews are not at all involved in the process of sifting and division characteristic of this age of the Ingathering of Exiles. We are, in fact (and even more, in consciousness), caught up in the centrifugal tendencies affecting the entire Jewish people.

But it is also of crucial significance that the sifting of the Jewish people in this age of the Ingathering of the Exiles has not taken a uniform course everywhere. It does not seem likely that all Jewish communities in the Diaspora will be liquidated within a foreseeable time, leaving behind everywhere outside of Israel only individual Jews incapable of carrying forward a community life. Emigration to Israel, far from having a significant effect on the American Jewish community, is so small that most people are hardly aware it exists. Even in other free democracies where a larger emigration to Israel is noted, the community is not appreciably affected by it. It is doubted, for that matter, that the emigration from North African countries in the next few years will exceed the natural increase of the Jews there, even though the liquidation of these Exiles is undoubtedly a possibility to be considered seriously today. Finally, behind the Iron Curtain are Jewries who are prevented by political obstacles from migration to Israel, though if it were possible it would be seized upon by masses as a veritable rescue. Thus the Ingathering of the Exiles in our time seems fated to be incomplete, and the Exile itself, though diminished and altered, seems fated to continue, but, at the same time, to exhibit certain centrifugal tendencies resulting from its involvement in the global Ingathering.

The Centrifugal Tendencies

Herzlian Zionism had planned that, when Jewish mass migration to Palestine became possible by international agreement, those Diaspora Jews who could not or did not wish to be assimilated would emigrate to the Jewish State, while the others would presumably disappear by assimilation. In this way, the Jewish problem would at last be solved. With the establishment of the Jewish State, the sifting of the Jewish people in the Diaspora has certainly begun. Even in the countries which, on the surface, seem unaffected by it, it has set in motion centrifugal tendencies and aroused anxiety about actual and apprehended divergences between Israel and the Diaspora.

Israel, establishing itself as a secular state, quite naturally has developed small ideological factions—notably the so-called Canaanites—that wish to draw rigid logical consequences from the separatist tendencies of the time. According to this view, Diaspora Jews who do not join the Ingathering, even if they fail to assimilate, should not be regarded as having any bond with Israel, for the fellowship of Israelis should be confined to the country's own borders. Such an attitude (if there were no more than logic to consider) is certainly compatible with a simplistic version of the classic Zionist ideology upon which Israel was founded, but its pragmatic consequences are such as the Israeli community as a whole could never contemplate. Even ideologically, not to speak of pragmatic consequences, Israeli Canaanitism is directly opposed to the neo-Zionist theory by which efforts are now being made to justify a permanent existence of the Diaspora.[1] Consequently, it is resented by many Western Jews perhaps even more bitterly than the revival of the ideology of assimilationism.

Though there may be only a few as self-conscious and as outspoken as Arthur Koestler, there are certainly a large number of Jews for whom the State of Israel has, in a certain sense, loosed bonds that held them to the Jewish people. Yet the rapid assimilation of the Jews appears impossible, owing, as we have seen, to an implicit theological argument about the historic condition of the Jews.[2] Even unbelieving Jews cannot easily bring themselves to adhere publicly to the anti-Semitic view of the divine rejection of the Jews. But this does not mean that such Jews always think their own people has the right of the matter in that debate. As a matter of fact, the prevailing Gentile view about Jewish religion is shared quite widely by Jews, increasingly so as their knowledge of Judaism declines. They, too, think that the higher ethical values of love and universal brotherhood came into the world only through Christianity and were not yet attained by Judaism. But such people are "prevented" by two reasons from converting in order to assimilate: first, the lack of any religious belief at all; second, a view characteristic even among non-religious Jews, that, whatever the abstract merits of Christian doctrine in the ethical realm, Christian practice toward the Jews shows that there is no substance in these protestations of Christian religion. Above all, conversion out of sheer expediency is impossible for the average decent unbelieving Jew. Even those cynical enough to pretend a belief they do not have may often be deterred by this consideration: when Jewry is under attack one cannot honorably join oneself to its attackers.

People of the kind described above really belong, under the standard conventions of the American Way of Life, to a fringe category, the category of the unchurched. By this negative definition is meant a nondescript grouping of citizens of the Republic who either do not bother or do not desire to identify themselves with the normal religious institutions in which American life centers, but for a part of their life, at least, exist somewhere outside these stable bounds. Among them, some may choose to congregate together in rather casual contacts, fostered particularly by big cities, and they may, if they wish, make this occasional association a surrogate for the community ties they have dropped. Under special conditions, as in the Greenwich Village bohemia, the association of marginal men may present a vivid simulation of true community. But the real social supports of such persons (if they still have any) remain the religious communities from which they sprang, for the Christians their Christian communities, and the Jews their Jewish community.

For Jews, this substitute community of the unchurched offers the nearest approach conceivable to full assimilation in the real America. For the Gentiles, on the other hand, it means a kind of bohemia in which to escape from too exigent demands of their native community. Obviously, it has a far greater potential social meaning for the Jews than for the

Gentiles. Despite this, the average Jewish unbeliever chooses the Jewish community, and not the surrogate community of marginal men, as that social identity wherein to live the most significant part of his life. To the extent the grounds of this choice become conscious, the decisive reason is not that the unbelieving Jew accepts the Jewish position on the theological dispute which is the underlying foundation of the Exile. The secular Jew chooses to be a Jew and reconciles himself to Jewishness because he shares, fully and directly, in the elementary Jewish *experience* of Exile. To overcome its crises and bring about whatever solution of its problems seemed to them best, such Jews have always willingly engaged their efforts and enthusiasm. Zionism was and remains one of the most significant forms in which the ties of these men with their Jewish community find a vivid expression.

The establishment of the State of Israel has not by far ended the significance of Zionism as a channel for identification with the Jewish community. Even a theorist as anxious to declare the Zionist movement defunct as Jacob B. Agus realizes that the loyalties it engendered still give meaning to Jewish life for many, many Jews who may, perhaps, not as easily respond to a particular institutional form of Jewish religion: "In any synthesis of national sentiments with religious values it is the latter that must be raised to the supreme level of importance; the former may be allowed but a subsidiary role, and encouraged only as they remain in accord with the standards and ideals of ethics and religion ... But when subordinated to higher considerations Jewish nationalism may continue to be a powerful creative force, serving the ends of Jewish religion, as it did in the past, by bringing to the aid of piety additional motivation, and by supplying foci of sentimental loyalty within the Jewish community."[3]

Jewish nationalism, it is needless to stress, still has many arduous tasks to perform. The solution which the State of Israel offers for the Jewish problem still remains sufficiently insecure, and, moreover, there are still so many in need who have not yet been able to profit by the Ingathering, that Zionism remains an obligation of the most pressing character upon the whole Diaspora. It will undoubtedly remain so for an untold time to come, for who can say when or at what boundary the Ingathering will be totally fulfilled? Yet the rise of the State of Israel has made one great difference in American Zionism. Until that great triumph, an American Zionist could always feel a personal fulfillment in Zionism, based on the assumption that he was building what could potentially become for him, too, literally his National Home. Now the State exists and opens its doors to him, and he finds himself faced all too unexpectedly with the decision: Is Israel really a Home to which he intends to go, no matter when, or is his migration not really something he even contemplates? The negative answer which most Zionists must give themselves when they ask this question at once depreciates the value of their personal indentification with the Zionist myth. This devaluation which they themselves carry out is reflected in a widening circle of discounts to which Zionism, as a binding force in the Jewish community, is subject among the wide fringe of its lukewarm or occasional sympathizers.

When the current of Zionist enthusiasm is stepped-down in power, the Jewish community loses one of the strongest attractive forces that made secular and semi-alienated Jews prefer to live their lives in the Jewish community rather than in the pseudo-community of marginal men. There is, on the other hand, a sociological force which is believed to be increasing the attraction of the community, and specifically of the synagogue. The trend of settlement to the suburbs brings Jews back into a *milieu* of tight and conventional community feeling.[4] On the strength of this development, there are many who think that the American Jewish community, on balance, is becoming more "integrated" than before, but one may venture the guess that together with the (recorded) growth of the synagogue, there is a growth (unrecorded) of the attraction for Jews of the marginal "society" of the unchurched and unsynagogued. It would not be surprising if in another generation the American Jewish community should show a very sharp increase in intermarriage rates. Already patterns of socializing among young college people indicate that, while intermarriage still remains low, young Jews do not feel convinced that it should necessarily be so. We recall the statistical picture of Jewish-Gentile intermarriage in Central Europe between the Wars which (together with low reproduction rates) led Jewish sociologists to conclude that, before Hitler appeared, these Jewries were already well on the way to biological submergence.[5]

Trends to Convergence

It would be foolish, of course, to forecast the ultimate effects of such tendencies to division and divergence in contemporary Jewry. If any balance sheet for a generation hence were to be made, then, certainly, the least it could conclude is that regardless of marginal loss (and always barring catastrophes) great Jewish communities will continue to exist in the Diaspora. Religious organization may be one force consolidating them, and the common experience of Exile will remain a pervasive element of underlying consensus, brought to the fore by pressing global Jewish tasks or local emergencies. Yet is is clear, too (as the new religious ideologists are very keenly aware), that these communities will show a serious division of their organized nuclei from their unorganized protoplasmic peripheries. Differing local conditions will also cause trends of divergence between one Diaspora community and another, as well as between Israel and the Diaspora. The urgent task of the moment is, accordingly, to reinforce every tendency that can counteract the centrifugal forces.

To this central problem of our times Dr. Kaplan has addressed himself with a marvelous pertinacity and attention to detail. In a recent book, he has made specific proposals whereby Israel and the Diaspora together, under the auspices of the World Zionist Organization, could overcome the present divisive tendencies.[6] These we should now like to consider.

The most important force for convergence, Dr. Kaplan feels, would be the self-dedication of the Israeli Jewish community to the task of serving as the spiritual home of Diaspora Jewry. In order to qualify itself for this function, Israel should adopt the following reforms: The Orthodox groupings and parties, the believers in supernaturalism and a total revelation at Mount Sinai, should become (or be forced to become?) tolerant of other, liberal, "this-worldly" forms of Jewish belief and practice, which should be established as the dominant style of religious culture of the Israeli Jews. On the other hand, the followers of the Socialist-Zionist Mapai party, the most representative group in the political and social life of the community, should redefine their existing principles and practices as constituting a religion, and as the authoritative continuation and revival (or may we say, reconstruction?) of the Torah, or at least of certain approved strands of Jewish tradition. All this should take place not in the course of a *Kulturkampf* but through a general conciliation of all parts of the community, wherein the present partisan groupings in Israel would be dissolved and a new consensus arise, binding all parts of Israeli Jewry to one another in a single religious brotherhood, and Israel to the traditions of the Exile and to the new Jewries of the Diaspora.

What Dr. Kaplan would like *Israel* to do on behalf of the religious reconstruction of the Jewish people, as outlined above, may be conceived as a remote, long-range ideal, which need not be incompatible with doing nothing, or very little, immediately to achieve it. For World Jewry, however, he proposes a step so direct and well-defined that one can either do it immediately, postpone doing it to a definite date, or reject it—but one cannot simply accept it "in principle." He wants no more and no less than for Zionism to convene a World Jewish Conference, a sort of Ecumenical Jewish Council. This assembly is to proclaim Jewry a world people, consecrated to a religious civilization, with its center in Israel, where the civilization is to flourish full-blown, and with its membership permanently domiciled throughout the world, where they will practice the tenets of the civilization as a cult. Following upon this proclamation, the Council will resolve itself into a permanent Institute (perhaps under the auspices of the Hebrew University) to study in detail the cultural, ritual, moral, and social-economic changes which the world Jewish community will have to institute in order to give substance to its Peoplehood.

If anyone in the Zionist leadership were led to take these proposals seriously and convened a World Conference for the sake of declaring the Jews a world People, a global religious brotherhood, one effect is certain: it would raise an unprecedented storm of controversy in the American Jewish community. The first to echo Dr. Kaplan's call might well be found among those who feel that Zionism in the Diaspora is now an outlived anomaly. The aims which they proposed to achieve under a banner of "non-Zionism" or impartial Jewishness they might welcome under Dr. Kaplan's banner of a "New Zionism." On the other hand, there are groups who have always reacted as a bull to a red flag whenever the idea of a formal unity of Jews is raised. We do not need to imagine their outcries, for they daily ring in our ears on far less provocation. As for the Zionists "in between," these typical American Jewish leaders who, as we have seen, today lean to Dr. Kaplan's basic ideas and use his language—they would be horrified not only at the prospect of arousing a controversy over formulas. They would be even more startled at being asked to commit themselves finally and definitely to all the consequences of a rhetorical phrase which happens at this moment to give them psychological comfort. Thus, the immediate effect of the attempt to convert Zionism into a general Jewish platform, upon which the whole Jewish people could converge, would be to bring about an explosion of differences that now lie dormant.[7]

The consequences of trying to give a uniform religious definition to Jewish Peoplehood and its world culture would be even more drastic. Among all the divisive factors in Jewish life today, there is none that can have so acute an effect as religious difference. Precisely because everyone is agreed —or well on the way to agreeing—that Jewish religious tradition, in its social and historical effects, is the bond that makes us One People, it would be fatal to try to arrive at formally binding agreements on religious issues, even in mere definition.

Dr. Kaplan should know this better than anyone else. It is he and his group whose reconstructed prayer book called forth the unique attempt at anathema and expurgation by a contemporary rabbinical group in America. What, then, would be the gale of protest that would follow an announcement by the labor groups and the liberal bourgeoisie of Israel and the Diaspora that they held their way of life, as exemplified particularly by the principles of the Histadrut, to be the authentic Jewish religion of our day? What practical man could be expected to accept a proposal to present this as the new essential Torah upon which to *unify* the Jewish People the world over?

Yet we cannot drop Dr. Kaplan in this way, by simply pointing out that his proposals are impractical. He is entitled to have us explain how so many American Zionists can accept his theoretical principles and yet reject their necessary practical conclusions.

This question leads us into areas where we maintain a precarious social equilibrium by a sort of conspiracy of silence. The American Jewish community keeps on a stable keel by not questioning too closely what we mean by Jewish religion. If Dr. Kaplan's proposals have been met with the indifference of a prudent sophistication or a wise skepticism, it is quite in keeping with the general non-seriousness that upholds this balance. Yet there is good reason to take Dr. Kaplan seriously, on his own terms, because the balance *is* a precarious one; and one, moreover, than can be maintained only at the price of cultural stultification.

If we must be frank, then, let us begin by being brutally frank. When American Zionists speak, as Dr. Kaplan does, of Israel as the spiritual home of the Jewish people; when, moreover, they demand that Israel's culture be "Jewish" so that they can share in it—there is only one way to describe that situation: the "culture" that is to be shared is a religion, and the relationship of Israel and the Diaspora is one of religious brotherhood. Yet there is nothing that could disturb American Jewry more than to attempt to formulate the substantive content of that "religion" and to specify the terms of that relationship. From this we can only infer that the theory of Israel as a spiritual home is clung to today by American Zionists not for what it implies if taken seriously (which is something they don't even wish to realize, for then the theory might have to be rejected), but only for the function it can fulfill, as an empty phrase, carefully guarded from ever acquiring specific content. All it means—or what it primarily means—is a convenient rhetorical dodge for answering Israelis when they demand that Zionists should come to Israel, and American non-Zionists when they ask us in what way we are different today from themselves.

That is one side, but only one side of the picture. Not only the polemical embarrassment of American Zionists, but the truly critical cultural and religious situation of both American and Israeli Jews demands today some sort of convergence on common cultural and religious values—and yet prevents that convergence from being formally concluded. Let us not talk about the situation in Israel. There is no need to stress how crucial is the need to find a "common ground" in culture for all the variegated Jewries congregating in the Homeland, or to reach some "synthesis" which will satisfy the Orthodox that the tradition is being loyally preserved and at the same time allow the free thinkers to retain their feeling that they too have a share in the Torah (as Ben-Gurion has put it). Nor need we labor the point that so long as Hebrew is the national language, Israel could not sever its ties with Jewish religion irrevocably even if it wished to; or stress the obvious fact that Israel is compelled quite deliberately to foster the Jewish individuality of its culture, if it is to attract immigrants whose main reason for coming must be that they cannot fully express themselves as Jews in the Diaspora. Let us rather give some attention to the cultural (or religious) dilemma of American Jewry, which has been far less frankly explored.

Nothing is more certain than that the secular culture advocated and nurtured by the American Jewish generation which preceded ours is now quite dead. In a way, the rise of the State of Israel struck the deathblow, or at least sounded the knell of its demise. Thus American Jewry, unless it clings to its religious tradition, is reduced to a sociological position similar to that of the Negro: Jewishness becomes a meaningless existential calamity. American Jews today want religion, because only through religion can they feel they *belong* in some positive, spontaneous sense, not merely by some mechanical sorting out of inconsiderate circumstance. But they can only take religion if it gives them what they want—that much and no more—and does not demand of them what they cannot give.

It is apparent that one of the things American Jews cannot give to religion is too specific, too doctrinal a faith. Ask any rabbi whether his congregation comes to him rather than to one of the other two Jewish "denominations" because of dogmatic differences! You will learn that social factors, tradition and habitudes, have far more to do with these choices. What this means is that all of the denominations are under pressure to meet certain general preferences of American Jewry as to ritual and practice, making them less and less different from each other. On the other hand, none of the denominations can afford to define its own final position on doctrine and practice too clearly. This is so for two reasons: first, because the adherents of each group belong to it not through conviction based on clear principles, but, by and large, by a balance of social preferences, which, moreover, shifts very easily; second, because any rigidity by one denomination could cause (particularly in the present atmosphere of religious revival) the others to become equally rigid in defense and raise the spectre of religious schism in Jewry.[8]

Thus American Jewry wants to believe, but it will not have what it believes too strictly defined. There is, moreover, a groundswell of religious convergence in American Jewry—but the ground it has to cover even to approach unity is vast. The cultural danger in which American Jewry stands today is a truly paradoxical one: it is the danger of taking our religious revival seriously enough to try to crystallize it in doctrine and deepen it in conception—and thus ask of American Jews a more specific faith than they are prepared to give; and it is also the danger that, as religious ardor rises and demands formulated belief, the groundswell of religious convergence will split on the reef of schism. Any attempt (even so liberal and non-committal a philosophy as Dr. Kaplan's) to formulate as "a religion" the cultural values that can bind Jews together and give meaning to their segregated social existence in America must necessarily have two effects: it rules out of the Jewish brotherhood that very large segment of the community that will not accept any explicit commitment to a religiously formulated belief; and it divides the "religionists" among themselves to the point where schism becomes imminent.

Israel enters into this paradoxical picture in a very curious way. We have seen how disinclined the American Zionists are to draw conclusions from their vaguely defined positions—and how right they are to be cautious. We could make precisely the same observation about the non-Zionists. If one were to define the logical extreme to which non-Zionism tends, it would be the thesis that American Jewry is not only a religious community, but a specifically American religious community. But it would be hard to find a non-Zionist who would defend this definition, for when examined with any degree of seriousness at all, such a position reveals itself as absurdly inadequate. The more one insists on the religious character of American Jewry, the less can one regard its essential beliefs as specifically American. There is certainly a minimum degree of universality which anything worthy of the name religion must not only claim but exhibit. In the case of Jewish religion, a claimant to that title must certainly show that it makes sense to (or at least has validity for) the Jews everywhere. Above all, any form of belief and practice that wishes to call itself Jewish is called upon to show that in Israel, the only community where Jews live on their own terms, there are some Jews who can identify themselves with it.

It is natural, therefore, that every form of Jewish religious belief in America (not to speak of Jewish secular "culturists") has shown a more or less acute awareness of the need to unite with Israel, at least to be represented there. The Orthodox Jews look to Israel with the highest (but also the most contradictory) expectations: sometimes that it will preserve, with a rigor not possible here, the full, fixed traditional way of life, and sometimes that it will establish a religious authority so respected and so trustworthy that it may dare to make necessary changes in the tradition. The non-Orthodox denominations look to the heterodoxically inclined or to the secular Jewish community in Israel for the development of new religious forms that will correspond at least in spirit to their own deviations from Orthodoxy. In addition to Dr. Kaplan, Reform and Conservative leaders alike are plainly anxious to establish not only a bridge to, but a bridgehead in, the State of Israel.[9]

Only on one condition can the American Jewish religious community, in its present condition of precarious unity and nebulous division, establish those religious-cultural ties with Israel that will give it the minimum assurance of universal validity which entitles it to be called religious: on condition that Israel does *not* accept any definition and canonization of its culture as religious, for in so doing it must necessarily exclude from the Jewish canon and declare schismatic (if not by intention, then inevitably in effect) all religious beliefs and denominations in American Jewry that define themselves differently from the Israelis. Only so long as Israel does not define its culture as a religion can American Jewry, as now constituted, retain a religious unity with it, each denomination and grouping in its own preferred fashion.

A Zionist Analysis

We find, then, that just as American Zionists are being pushed by logic to recognize their cultural bond with Israel as really a quasi-religious cult, so the American Jewish religious denominations are being pushed by logic and events to seek a bond with Israel. Yet to try to crystallize and formulate the conclusions to which conditions point, as Professor Kaplan proposes, would precipitate the fatal divisions that inhere in that very bond wherein we seek unity.

What shall we call this situation? Is it an "inherent contradiction" that must be resolved, or one of those problems that one does not solve, but tries to live with? How shall we regard those who try to preserve it? As fainthearted and hypocritical, or as wisely empirical?

This is, indeed, the unsatisfactory crux to which we are driven if we assume that, because the Jewish problem arises ultimately from a theologico-historical disagreement, we must frame a solution in specific religious terms. But whatever the *ultimate* cause of Jewish existence, Jewishness also is an experience shared by all Jews, no matter what the form of their belief or disbelief. The substance of that experience has been until now the Exile. It now includes also the Ingathering of the Exiles, whether as a direct or a vicarious experience, as well as the erratic progress of that Ingathering and the unexpected obstacles with which it is confronted, with the probable prospect that the Ingathering (for the foreseeable future) is fated to remain incomplete. As an experience, this is certainly complex, even paradoxical—but hardly lacking in vividness and tension. To try to reduce it to a doctrine leads, not only, as we have seen, to insoluble contradictions. The bias of the doctrines proposed is precisely to blur the central Jewish experience itself; for the substance of it is Exile and the effort to be redeemed from it, and the new doctrines arise out of a need to repress the sense of Exile because we no longer want to be redeemed from it.

Whatever may be the case with small groups of extremists, it seems incontrovertible that for the average American Jews the contemporary American Jewish problem is not the kind of problem that one would seek to solve. It is rather the kind of problem that he must try to live with. If we were called upon to solve the problem, then we could favor a clear and simple doctrine, even if it did violence to experience. But when we are required to live with a problem, then the clear and simple rationalizations of it serve only to repress the understanding that is actually needed. For the first necessity is to see truly and give a sincere account of our authentic being.

The American Jewish situation sets us a problem so equivocal in its terms that to live with it almost inevitably involves a compromise of principle. For whatever clear principle may be adopted, even, as we have seen, a principle which ardently seeks to naturalize Jewishness and adapt it to the American Way of Life, to live by it with rigorous consistency would involve a drastic alteration of existing conditions. Yet this hardly means that the average American Jew will encounter any real difficulty in living with the Jewish problem in America. To make compromises, to relativize absolutes, to circumvent principle with practicalities, is a faculty everyone acquires in the course of growing up. The rare human being who reaches maturity unable or unwilling to put up with compromise may be burdened with an exceptional sensitivity and rigorous conscience or he may simply be emotionally retarded. Undoubtedly, to learn to hedge is always hard for the innocent, and even for the mature man it often goes against the grain. Fortunately—or unfortunately, as the case may be—the compromises required of American Jews in our contemporary situation are quite easily made.

The least common denominator to which the American Jewish problem may be reduced (as we noted earlier) expresses itself in what is undoubtedly a question of notable insignificance, to wit: since short-run assimilation is improbable and most Jews will have to remain Jews, willy nilly, what is there that can be preserved or worked up in the way of Jewish culture, or Jewish religion, to make being a Jew seem worthwhile?[10] This is surely the most vulgar formulation of a collective will to live that has ever been proposed, but it happens to express a mood that has its crucial importance in the American Jewish situation.

A passion for Jewishness which can express itself in this fashion is very easily fulfilled. At such a minimum degree of intensity, the need for Jewish culture is "adequately" satisfied by a fetishistic cult, by the empty symbols of a culture. The most available symbols are, of course, those of the synagogue and of Jewish religious culture. So long as a Jewish community maintains a rabbi and some form of religious service, it has justified its separate existence well enough for purposes of public relations, and in terms familiar to the American Way of Life. It is up to the rabbi and a few synagogue habitués to vouch for the Jewish authenticity of the substance that lies behind these public symbols. What is implied by such a situation emerges from an example that is, perhaps, anecdotal, but certainly characteristic of the low point from which the reconstruction of Jewishness in second and third generation America has often had to begin. The story is told of a Jewish community that had always had daily prayer maintained by a *minyan* of ten old men. One, however, reached a ripe old age and passed away, making regular communal prayer impossible unless the community supplied the necessary tenth. None of the mature men could spare time from his business for this symbolic service, and the community stood in danger of losing a recognized emblem of Jewishness. The problem was solved in a characteristic way: as each boy in the community reached the age of *bar mitzvah* he was obliged to join the *minyan* until relieved by the next thirteen-year-old to reach ritual maturity. In this way, traditional Jewishness was preserved by a union of dependent generations, too old or too young to have more serious obligations and able, therefore, to devote themselves to the care of the community fetish.

If this (or, in the case of a Reform community the same situation in another form) is the rock-bottom minimum from which the synagogue must try to reconstruct Jewishness, it is clear what is the most immediately important Jewish task. The elementary basis for the revival of American Jewishness may be the awareness that Jews must be Jews whether they like it or not, and its beginning may be the discovery that the religious forms of Jewishness are both respected by Gentiles and pliable enough to be made comfortable for any Jewish taste. But it is essential to bring the Jewish revival to a further stage, without which it remains neither secure nor significant. The easy, compromising, trivially symbolic Jewishness of the first stage of the revival must begin to mean something serious and profoundly personal at least to some of the Jews, or they will be unable to carry it on.

As it happens, those Jews who need a profound conviction in order to function in the community are the most essential to its continuation. Thus, one of the most striking features of the present Jewish religious revival has been the sharp rise in personal piety and theological concern that has been noted among rabbis. And certainly one cannot expect to attract young people to a religious belief on the grounds that it is a social convenience. If the Jewish community were to try to maintain itself solely on this basis, each generation, as it grows into maturity, would have to be exposed to the shock of learning through personal experience that social conditions *force* one to be a Jew. Only after facing reality in this cold, hard shape can anyone agree to adopt a

Judaism experienced as no more than the attractive, stylized fittings of what is basically regarded as a prison.

However, to live in a Jewish religious community as a social convenience means that one is ultimately compelled (not, perhaps, the particular individual but individuals in crucial social situations within the community; hence, the communty at large) to face Judaism as a serious matter. A Jewish community which defines itself as religious challenges a severe test, the test of really being religious. The religious culture of Judaism may be accepted, at first, in a superficially attractive form, simply because anyone would want to "like" being a Jew if he has to be a Jew anyway. But, in the final analysis, one cannot accept Judaism, or any serious religious commitment, simply because one "likes" it; one has to "mean" it. This is a test that a great part of the community may evade, relying on the authority of those religious specialists who stand as the symbolic embodiment of Jewish faith. But it is a test which not only the religious functionaries but all young Jews, as they face the crisis of maturity, must undergo; and the more sensitive and intelligent they are, the more profoundly it must concern them.

Religious faith, in our day, has become defined as a rather special experience. We do not mean by this simply the fact that in all religions only a few men endeavor to live at a continuously high pitch of personal devotion, while the mass accept religion as given to them in impersonal traditional forms, and even experience personal religious exaltation only through established collective rites. What we refer to is that, through the spread of the world religions over a variety of cultural areas, religion has come to be a compartment of life, with its own ecclesiastical culture and institutions. The mass of the people set aside a part of their lives, separated from their regular pursuits and secular culture, for the practice of sacred rites, in holy places and on special occasions. The religious virtuosos withdraw from the regular pursuits of life and reject the values of secular culture in order to devote themselves entirely to the values of a holy existence. The vastly increased scope and significance of secular culture in modern times has challenged the claim of religious culture upon certain realms of knowledge or of life that it previously dominated, and has even occasionally challenged the validity of all religion. But, it is not secularism that originated the relegation of religion to a compartment of life; this was brought about much earlier by the spread of world religions beyond the sphere of any single ethnic culture.

Since Jewish religion never succeeded in establishing itself beyond the bounds of its ethnic group, Jewish religious culture did not become a segregated compartment of Jewish culture. Obviously, this does not deny that Jewish religion, too, specified certain particularly sacred places and occasions and holy practices, nor that it always had religious virtuosos who devoted themselves to a life of intense devotion. But Jewish religious culture was essentially one with its whole "profane" way of life; not a rejection of it nor segregated from it but rather a continuous quality that ran through all of Jewish life, sometimes in a rarefied, sometimes in a condensed and materialized, form. Jewish life as a whole, not just a compartment of it, was holy and devoted, for through the conception of Exile and Chosenness it stood apart from the profane history of the world and rejected its actual values.

Accordingly, the authentic Jewishness of Jewish religion seems to have depended, as a general rule, on Exile's being not a mere word, but an actual condition. Wherever Jews lived in effective segregation, whether territorial or social, and communicated with Gentile society and Gentile values as one integral group with another—that is, through processes which are suggested by such words as ingestion, translation, and exchange rather than assimilation, communion, and sharing—they lived lives and produced culture that could be thoroughly imbued with the spirit of their religion. But wherever Jewish segregation broke down and the average Jew (not just the representative of the Jews) shared a major part of his life with Gentiles, then Jewish religion began to be a separate compartment of life and culture and no longer enjoyed an integral relation with the Jews' secular values.

[143

Symptomatic effects of this situation have always been these two tendencies: first, the authority to change Jewish religious folkways was now no longer inherent in social development, because so much of social life was lived outside of Jewish traditions; secondly, Jewish folkways no longer were accepted simply because everyone followed them and their forms seemed endowed with a natural fitness, but we were urged to observe them because our ancestors had followed them at God's behest and, however arbitrary they might appear, they had the virtue of inducting one into a separate ecclesiastical culture of holiness.

The Americanization of Jewish life, like all other trends of secularizing the Jew, has meant, above all, reducing Jewish religion to a mere compartment of life. This happened to a community whose religious culture (particularly in the case of the Ashkenazic Jews) had been built upon a far-reaching segregation from the Gentiles and had consequently been so intimately interwoven with its ethnic culture that not until recent times could the two be distinguished at all.

When a Jew with this background must face seriously his commitment to Jewish religion in its reduced circumstances, he finds that only by restoring it to something like its old, authentic context can he make his Jewishness mean anything to him. Only a Jewish religion that goes against the stream and seeks to recapture what has been lost can be taken seriously as either Jewish or religious.

The two ways in which it is proposed to bring the present religious revival to a secure conclusion, and to make real Jews out of symbolic Jews, both lead toward restoring a context of Jewish ethnic culture, though unfortunately neither one leads far enough, or sees clearly where it is leading. One way—we may call it the right-wing or neo-Orthodox way—asks us to adopt the traditional Jewish folkways on faith, just as we should accept God.[11] This view stresses that the traditional ways were the medium whereby our fathers lived a pious and holy life, and if we submit ourselves to them lovingly and patiently they can bring us moments of realized holiness, too. But Jewish neo-Orthodoxy (like all neo-Orthodoxies) cannot mask the difference between our situation and our fathers' situation. For our fathers, the ancient folkways were by no means as arbitrary as they must seem to us, but they were rather the natural outer expression befitting a self-sufficient communal life. The whole of a Jew's life was attuned to these rites. Consequently, the tradition was free to grow. Even if we create ghettoes for ourselves, we cannot provide this kind of natural environment for Jewish Orthodoxy in America, for so great a part of every Jew's life here is passed outside the scope of Jewish culture.

Moreover, the ideological bias of *neo*-Orthodoxy is to defend the naturalization of Judaism in America—that is, to seek to repress our awareness that American Jews are in Exile —even though its adherents are consciously engaged in building themselves a spiritual ghetto for the religious compartment of their lives. But that the Jewish cult has not really been naturalized in America is implicit not only in the actions but in the very line of argument the neo-Orthodox adopt. For they ask us to accept without alteration a Judaism that *other* Jewries have defined. The tradition neo-Orthodoxy recommends is derived from communities whose Jewishness pervaded their whole lives, so that they were entitled to innovate. We here, whose Judaism has been reduced to a cult, can only observe what they handed down to us and trust that it may bring us from mechanical piety to moments of elevation. Thus, because we are not in a secular exile, we cannot make ourselves at home in our Jewishness, for we dare not bend it to fit our lives. The more fully one enters into the Orthodox frame of mind, the more one must realize that only a community fully Jewish in its secular life can sustain a living, growing Jewish religious culture, an Orthodoxy which is not a neo-Orthodoxy, one which lives by its own religious intuition and not by consulting other models. Every neo-Orthodoxy must look to a genuine Orthodoxy as its guide. Neo-Hassidism in Germany looked to the full-blooded Jewish community in Eastern Europe for inspiration. Today, neo-Orthodoxy must ultimately come to regard Israel and the self-sufficient Jewish community there as the true home of the authentic, living Jewish tradition—and to realize that American neo-Orthodoxy lives in Exile.

The second way—we may call it the left-wing or progressive way—to bring the religious revival to a more adequate consummation is to try to relate Jewish religious culture once more to the values of the secular life of the contemporary American Jew. American Jewish religious observances have already, for the most part, been altered so that they accord with what seems fitting and natural to a Jew attuned to American standards of propriety. But what is essential is for the extra-synagogal life of the Jew to conform to characteristic principles of Jewish tradition. Even Christianity, which preceded American Jewry by so many centuries in building an ecclesiastical culture by separation from the profane life, must make some attempt to bring extra-ecclesiastical life into conformity with Christian standards if it takes itself seriously. But for Christian churches this task is far simpler than it can possibly be for contemporary Jewish religious ideologists. Our society *is* a Christian society, and however secularized, reliance upon Christian values, or at least respect for them, is built into its very structure. For this very reason, Jewish ideology cannot relate our religious culture to secular values which Jews have simply adopted from life in a Gentile environment. To the extent any attitude to *Judaism* is built into this life, it is usually a rejection of Judaism. The effort to give substance to Jewish religion by giving it a secular expression leads, therefore, to exhortations that Jews should *distinguish* themselves from the Gentiles, by exemplary conduct in accordance with such (mainly ethical) principles of Jewish tradition as the reformed or reconstructed Judaism approves.[12]

The bias of this ideology, too, is to defend the naturalization of Judaism in America. Consequently, it denies the Exile, and must look elsewhere for a rationalization of the distinction which it urges upon the Jews. The usual solution is to stress the Chosenness of the Jews, their collective Mission and calling, as the reason why their secular lives must be different from the Gentiles'. However, having sought to blind itself to the true and tangible source of Jewish difference, the national history of Exile, the Mission theory takes refuge in such palpably empty and vainglorious pretensions to distinction that it is difficult for anyone but a preacher or an ideologist to take them seriously—which is to say they cannot have the desired effect, namely, to give substance to the so far merely symbolic revival of Jewish religion.[13]

Eventually, this ideological tendency, too, is driven to realize that Jewish religious culture cannot find a true secular expression except in a community whose secular life is fully Jewish. Mordecai M. Kaplan does not care to hear the word "Exile" applied to American Jews. But he implicitly concedes the point, when he looks to contemporary Israel for the substantial secular values through which Jewish religious culture can express itself, and which can provide a model of authentic Jewishness for the sustenance of a reconstructed Jewish cult in America.

If this analysis is correct, then the logic of the contemporary anti-Zionist and neo-Zionist positions leads to the conclusion that Israel alone can develop a really authentic Jewishness in our time. It is upon one or another form of Jewishness as practiced in Israel that each ideology would have to rely, if it faced the actual situation squarely. But to face the actual situation squarely is precisely what these ideologies refuse to do. For the most general and fundamental characteristic of the Jewish situation, in contemporary America as everywhere else in the Diaspora throughout history, is Exile. Exile, to be sure, is an experience imposed upon Jews because of the history of the Jewish religion, but it is Exile rather than religion which is today the basic experience common to all Jews in the Diaspora and which is capable of bringing them all into communion. This is especially so after a century and a half of secularization and mass migration that have divided the Jews religiously and estranged so many of them from all positive religion. Yet, however estranged from Jewish tradition, all Jews share the special Jewish experience of Exile, and there is nothing that can so readily bring the values of Jewish culture home to them as the manifold profound and beautiful elaborations of this theme in every form of traditional Jewish expression.

Exile is precisely the value and experience that the new ideologies quite consciously seek to repress (though they cannot do so successfully—as we have seen—if they take their own positions as seriously as they ultimately must). They argue that the doctrine of Exile is a pessimistic doctrine which cannot encourage Jews to build Judaism in America. As we have seen, this was certainly the reverse of the truth in the period before the State of Israel was founded. Precisely in the concept of Exile, by which the Jewish problem is conceived on a historic scale transcending contemporary America, and in the enthusiasm of trying at long last, to overcome Exile through Zionism, did Jews find the confidence to swim against the stream of American pressure and build a Jewishness more authentic, if less convenient, than we now dare to hope for. However, we have also noted the decline in morale resulting from the abrupt realization of Zionism and the possibility offered to Jews (at least, *de jure*) to end the Exile for themselves in the most direct and immediate way. When so many Zionists proved unable or unwilling to avail themselves of this opportunity, there was naturally a pressure upon them to give up the doctrine of Exile itself. For surely it is mere perversity (unless it were a penitential rite adopted by a religious virtuoso) to cling to Exile when one is offered redemption. One outlet offered to Jews in this dilemma is the Koestler theory proposing assimilation, but this is hardly practicable for many. The new theories seeking to repress the awareness of Exile make a natural appeal to those for whom Koestler's solution is unavailable. The appeal is especially great, naturally enough, to those who still maintain some kind of attachment to Jewish religion. Yet despite the apparent popularity of the new theories, repression of the sense of Exile neither is necessary nor it is as widespread as might be supposed. The Zionists, cowed by their own "inconsistency," have not let themselves be heard, but this does not mean they have all been convinced by the new doctrines. In this first period of ideological readjustment they simply lack the courage of their own convictions. But many of them are far from ready to persuade themselves that they are no longer in Exile, simply because they could not, or would not, avail themselves personally of the chance to be redeemed from it. Well-founded convictions do not yield quite that easily to psychological convenience in the average man.

What is certainly not true is that it is necessary to repress the sense of Exile in order to be an effective force for a more authentic Jewishness in America. No Jewishness that can be taken seriously is possible in America without going counter to convenience, and without grasping the Jewish question in a historic frame that transcends the contemporary American situation. The most significant movement in the contemporary course of Jewish history is the Ingathering of the Exiles to Israel. That this is proceeding in piecemeal fashion and that major Diaspora communities, and particularly American Jewry, seem fated to participate in it only vicariously or through exceptional representatives, is not determined solely by the unwillingness of Diaspora Zionists to be redeemed (though this obviously determines why many particular individuals do not migrate). Even if every American Zionist were fully resolved to move to Israel at once, objective difficulties and limitations would cause a long time to pass before more than a small fraction could accomplish this desire. But whether willing or unwilling, able or unable, to emigrate, every Zionist who participates even vicariously in the Ingathering of the Exiles shares more fully in the spirit—and often enough in the substance—of the nuclear Jewish experience growing up today in Israel than one who tries to repress its significance.

We have seen that to share somehow in the global experience of the Jewish people and particularly in the values natural to the fully Jewish community in Israel is essential (despite any reservations that may properly be made) to any ideology that might be proposed for Jewish life in America. The Zionist who refuses to repress his sense of Exile is, to this extent at least, able far more directly and easily than any other to contribute positively to the maintenance of Jewishness in America. But it is, of course, part of an awareness of Exile to know that a living Jewish culture cannot in

[149

the truest sense be sustained as a cult away from its native soil. Whoever most intensely needs to participate in the life of this culture will inevitably be drawn to Israel, whether he actually go there or not.

It is a logic without human penetration which would conclude that because of this such persons would become slack in trying to maintain an authentic Jewishness in America. A psychologically sensitive logic would understand, as experience has shown, that such persons, more demanding in their standards of Jewishness and less content with what can be conveniently achieved, may be precisely the ones who are ready to make the special efforts that the goal of an authentic Jewishness requires anywhere in the Exile.

Coda and Finale:
The Jewish Mission

There is a certain pathos in the attempts made by all the ideologies defending the permanency of Diaspora communities to resuscitate the idea of the Jewish Mission. After the Zionist critique of this conception, contemporary versions of it must begin by repudiating a number of its apparent implications. Kaplan, Gordis, Agus, Horace Kallen and Waldo Frank all deny that the Jews are a Chosen People if this means that they alone have received a true Revelation, or are racially or in any other way inherently superior to other peoples.[14] Nor can it be the peculiar Jewish Mission, they realize, for the Jews to stand witness to values and ideas which are common to Christianity and Islam as well. The Jewish Mission is conceived by them, rather, as a distinction which Jews must bear with consecration, and perhaps even through suffering, because they remain true to values and ideas *different* from those of the majority. Yet the attempt to define just what are the values and ideas which mark the Jew as different from the majority leads all these thinkers, however diverse their points of departure, to a common difficulty: at bottom, the differences which they defend are really an expression of the fundamental Jewish historical experience of Exile; yet it is precisely in order to deny or discount the fact of Exile that their theories have been devised.

Orthodoxy does not suffer from this embarrassment. First of all, it knows quite clearly what the values and ideas are that consecrate the Jews as different. They are the Revealed Law of God and the authoritative interpretations of it in Jewish tradition. Secondly, a key concept in that tradition is the Jewish divinely ordained history of Exile and Redemption. But when one has adopted the notion of a continuous revelation, implying that history is the organ wherein truth emerges, then one can no longer rely on the past, on authority and tradition, to justify difference. The values and ideas that make one different must seem valid contemporaneously—which means they must have a felt significance, either in the present or at least for the future.

We have noted how ill at ease Kaplan and Agus, Kallen and Frank are about the present state of Jewish ideas and values.[15] They are actively concerned both to withstand the inroads of present pressures upon values inherited from the past and to revise traditions that have lost value so that they may be better adapted to our times. But there is another reason, too, why the actual character of Jewish difference, both in the present and the past, makes them uneasy. What Jews are today, and have been for two thousand years, is all too clearly determined by one fundamental historic condition, the Exile. These writers are aware of the overpowering significance of this "negative" fact in the collective historic experience of the Jews; but it is hard for them to accept frankly the impermanence which it implies as a basic element in the matrix of facts and values that actually make Jews today "different."

Mordecai Kaplan is concerned that a Jewish education which builds upon the collective Jewish experience of Exile will "have a ruinous effect on the happiness and character" of Jewish children and lead to the development of psychoneuroses. At the same time, he is fully aware of the powerful and pervasive effects of the consciousness of Exile upon Jewish culture and Jewish personality. He knows very well that the source of the condition of Exile is the Jewish-Christian

[151

quarrel about the place of the Jews in the divine drama of history. He repudiates that quarrel, and is even bold enough to propose an agreement among world churches to abolish the beliefs and rituals which perpetuate it. As far as the Jews are concerned, he proposes a unilateral renunciation of the Chosen People concept. Instead, he proposes that the Jews consider themselves to have a "vocation." This rather verbal change nevertheless has two effects: it reduces the mythic proportions of Jewish "difference" to a status which any other people or religion can also claim—thus, the Exile is to be exorcised; and it places the divinity of Jewish historical experience (as of all other revelations) not in any past or present source but in the perpetual future.[16]

The other writers present much the same picture. All realize the central historical importance of what Dr. Agus, in acute discomfort, calls the "meta-myth"—the Jewish idea of their divine Election and Exile, and the Gentile idea of the Jewish Rejection. All would like to reduce or transform it (as far as Jews are concerned) from a historical fatality to a self-assumed mission, from an actuality of the past and present to a vocation toward the future, and from a cosmically and historically unique status to an individual difference as normal as any other. All, too, would like the Christians to transform their own picture of the Jew in the same way, but none is ready to make this demand as specifically and with as much apparent confidence as Dr. Kaplan.[17]

Thus, on the one hand, all these authors are exceedingly anxious to make both Jews and Christians abandon the traditional myth-images of providential history through which each has understood the nature and source of difference between Jews and Christians. Some, like Dr. Kaplan, are bold enough to propose a deliberate reconstruction of traditions to eliminate these conceptions from both Judaism and Christianity. Others, like Dr. Kallen, can only sadly suggest such wisdom, with no real belief that it can actually be attained today. But the main stress of all alike is on something more "positive." They devote most of their attention to promoting a new consensus of Jewish-Christian understanding, based on one or another formulation of ideas "everyone" accepts (monotheism, the emergent God, or even "secularism" as "the religion of religions," the common search for truth through liberty). Through this approach, Judaism would become one of many facets of an identical historically revealed core of truth; not, as in the old conception, the reverse (elected or rejected) side of the same coin. It becomes the mission of Israel to help the whole truth be revealed by giving full, free, and authentic expression to its own, particular historic experience of it.

There are two ways in which these authors envisage the mission of Israel to reveal its own particular truth in the Diaspora. The first is an intellectual way, the way of individual scholars and creators. The second is a historical, experiential way, the way of the entire community. The first way is a true and authentic possibility for Jews in the Diaspora, while the second is today largely pretense, and, under present conditions, will remain so: such is the conclusion to which our analysis has led us.

We have already considered the view that the function of Jewish culture is to produce spontaneous individual aesthetic expressions, rooted in alienation and unable to establish a continuous tradition.[18] Obviously, the rabbis among our ideologists cannot be satisfied with this. They, too, stress scholarship and creative artistry as a primary form for expressing the Jewish difference, but since they concern themselves with defending the distinctive Jewish tradition and reconstructing its principles, they postulate a continuing relationship of the creative individual with the Jewish community. In fact, however, even the creativity which the rabbis advocate and represent, as an expression of the Jewish difference and "vocation," is related authentically only to the past of our Jewish culture and community; its relationship to the future of the community is a pretense, or, if you prefer, a preachment.

There is an authentic and significant contribution Jewish scholarship can make, and is making, to general culture by re-examining the history of ideas from the specific Jewish vantage point. The Jews have been in the extraordinary position of sharing more or less intimately the entire development of modern man from the origins in Mediterranean antiquity, through the Moslem-Jewish-Christian medieval civilization, to the rise of Western civilization. Yet throughout it all they have been segregated in greater or lesser degree and have maintained an independent tradition. That this tradition, an authentic part of Western cultural history, is virtually unknown to Gentiles means that our account with the past is significantly incomplete. Jewish scholarship, using new materials and taking an independent viewpoint unencumbered by the traditional Gentile preconceptions, can open up new vistas to our general culture.[19]

This was impossible so long as Jewish scholarship remained insulated from Gentile culture and considered only its own specific problems. But even after Jewish scholars learned to apply Gentile methods and Gentile materials to their own problems, there remained another obstacle. Jewish scholarship remained largely apologetic in character, confining itself to an exposition of Jewish topics by standard critical methods, with the double aim of reforming the Jewish tradition and defending it from Gentile misunderstanding.

Dr. Gordis is undoubtedly right when he rejects a contention frequently heard in Zionist literature, that in the Diaspora Jewish scholarship must always remain inherently apologetic; that only in Israel can it speak freely about Gentile as well as Jewish topics.[20] Certainly, mature Jewish scholars in the Diaspora can make and have made remarkable contributions to our knowledge not only of Jewish but of Gentile tradition by using the materials and point of view available to them as Jews. Moreover, Gentile scholars critical of their own tradition have increasingly found in a new appreciation of the Jewish tradition, learned from modern Jewish scholarship (both Diasporic and Israeli), insights and examples supporting new trends in their own Christian culture.[21]

But when the new ideologists claim that Catholic Israel, as a collective entity still creating its tradition anew, is or will be productive of new insights and new values arising from the specific Jewish contemporary situation in the

Diaspora (the situation which they refuse to face frankly as one of alienhood and Exile, but recognize as one of difference), and that for the sake of these potential social values it is worthwhile being a Jew—this we cannot take seriously. We can (most of us, at least) accept it easily enough as an ideological justification for a social fact which is bound to exist in any case; but this is the kind of ideology which is sheer verbalizing, totally without mythic force. To the extent it suggests we should do something not forced upon us anyway by circumstances it can have no effect. For what (if one represses the awareness of our global, historic Exile) is the social reality of Jewish collective experience in America out of which the new values are to arise? A positive Jewishness centered in the synagogue, when the synagogue itself does not articulate our historic consciousness of Exile, is based on a social herding together of Jews who can sustain no more than a culture of fetishes whose purported value only a hieratic group of functionaries can decipher. What more than this can any culture contribute if its creativity can draw on no more social substance than synagogue attendance—and even that as infrequent and superficial as is characteristic of American Jewry? To be sure, there is more social substance to Jewish life in America than this description suggests. But that is because so much of our Jewish life here centers around institutions, other than the synagogue, where the Exile is much more frankly faced.

If Jewish culture still has new values to offer the world at large, it will be proved only in a place where Jewish social existence faces new, real, serious problems. Despite all ideological pretenses, no one really doubts that it is in Israel alone that this essential condition obtains.

We cannot conclude without a final word. After so lengthy a criticism of other solutions and other ideologies regarding the contemporary Jewish problem in America, how does a secular Zionist positively assess his situation? What proposals, if any, would he make? The situation, let us recall, is one in which, after the establishment of the Jewish State, the Ingathering of the Exiles seems fated to remain incomplete and major Diaspora communities seem destined to persist. The specific question we must answer is this: How do we view the situation, or what do we propose, in regard to the great community of American Jews who are, and no doubt will remain, unaffected by the Ingathering into Zion?

Whatever *solution* Zionism has to offer for the Jewish problem must necessarily inhere in the movement from the Diaspora to Israel.[22] That solution has been complete for some communities, for others it is still in process, and will remain so, in all likelihood, for many, many years to come. We do not foresee yet the moment at which we will sense that the solution of the Jewish problem will have gone as far as it need or can go. As long as it continues in process, the Ingathering of the Exiles fills the Jewish life of every Zionist in Israel, going to Israel, or even prevented from going to Israel with meaning always serious and frequently exigent.

Where a Jewish community seems destined to remain in Exile, Zionism offers no *solution* for its problems; but, for that matter, neither does any other philosophy which hopes to see the Jews survive. In this case, the Jewish problem becomes a problem to live with, not a problem to solve. Whoever has become a Zionist (even before the State was established—or, perhaps, *especially* before the State was established) has also, in that very fact, found a new way to live with the Jewish problem. He has learned a way to belong to the Jewish community, if he had not known any way previously; and if he always knew that he was a Jew, his Jewishness has acquired a new vitality. By the establishment of the State of Israel and the new pride it instilled in all Jews, Zionism (as Isaiah Berlin has pointed out) made it easier for non-Zionists to live with the Jewish problem: it reduced the dimensions of the problem.[23] At the same time, however, for the Zionist prevented from participating in the Ingathering directly it made the Exile more rather than less difficult to bear, for it was now an Exile, in principle, self-imposed. Yet nothing was altered, even for him, in essentials: a Zionist continued to find a vital meaning in his belonging to the Jewish people through being a Zionist.

A secular Zionist is one who experiences the common modern conviction that God-consciousness is a personal, not a social matter. Only through a profound personal commitment to God, such as is commended to us by neo-Orthodox ideologists like Abraham J. Heschel and Will Herberg, could he accept a religious communion. Failing such a personal commitment, he no doubt remains Jewish, like all other Diaspora Jews, owing ultimately to the Jewish-Christian quarrel over the nature of divine history and the place of the Jews in it. No more than the new non-Orthodox religious ideologists can he accept the traditional myth (or "meta-myth") of the Exile, nor commit himself to it. But Zionism gives his Jewishness sufficient vitality so that he need not, and his non-committed religiosity means that he cannot, resort to the new religious ideologies which seek to repress the fact of Exile through its sublimation into an insubstantial "vocation."

The attitude of the secular Zionist to the Jewish religious tradition must obviously be different from that of a committed "religionist." That he is a secular and not a religious Jew means he has not experienced such a religious commitment to Jewish culture as would make it, for him, not only a profound but a most personal revelation of God. This does not mean he is unable to appreciate the expressions of an urge towards divinity in it or in other religious cultures. Nor does it mean that his relation to Jewish religious culture is a neutral or indifferent one. Certainly as a culture, if not as a religion, it has an intimate personal meaning for him, and there is no collective tradition in which he is more disposed to find expressions of divinity that speak to him personally. But he cannot adopt it as a norm, nor as a certain, unfailing, and least of all exclusive revelation of God.

He may hope that, in Israel, the liberated Jewish religious impulse may lead to new revelations of divinity. But, as a secularist, there are certain things he cannot do. He cannot accept a Jewish religious ideology simply because he is a Jew, for he will only be converted as a human before God. Nor can he undertake to be a Jew only to the extent he is religious, or have impulses to religion only as a Jew.

These are the bounds whose crossing would make him no longer a secularist.

How does such a secular Zionist live with the Jewish problem in America? As we have noted, he belongs to the Jewish people with a vital attachment inherent in Zionism. The Exile is a condition not veiled from him by scented mists of ideology which would make it seem a facile "vocation," nor is it a stern commitment which seems to him divine; it is a fate whose religious justification has vanished, and which has now acquired a specific, pragmatic significance through the Zionist resolve to overcome it. To participate in the continuing Zionist effort at a solution gives vitality to one's Jewish "belongingness," for it sets the Diaspora Zionist high and demanding tasks. He is committed to the effort to preserve Jewish culture in the Diaspora on a level that will maintain an adequate national consensus in the continuing Ingathering—a level far higher than is considered necessary for the kind of Jewish culture that proposes to exist permanently in the Diaspora, but none too high, by the way, to provide the informed leadership that even such a program requires.

Whoever is enabled by such Zionism to live with the Jewish problem in America has undoubtedly made his own problem more acute. Whatever obstacles and difficulties may exist for him, the fact that the doors of Israel are open to him means that, in a sense, his Exile is self-imposed. Sheer intellectual honesty may prevent him from accepting any of the easily available ideological evasions of this fact. But his own intellectual position is one that can only be passed on to those younger people who can resolve, for themselves, to end the Exile and join the Ingathering. In a sense, it has no natural place in the American Jewish community, for it is based on the "unnatural" (but authentically Jewish) assumption that American Jewry is impermanent. But the ideologies which do have a "natural" and "functional" place in American Jewry and which assume its permanence are based on intellectual contrivances that recommend themselves more by their convenience than by their moral and intellectual cogency.

158]

The Exile is too serious an experience for the most serious and sensitive young people to hide from themselves. There will always be many found among them for whom, as for Jewish secularists of earlier generations, only secular Zionism can give meaning and vitality to Jewishness in our time. So too there will always be many young religious Jews whom awareness of Exile will bring to Zionism. But Zionism faces the Exile, first and foremost, as a problem to be solved, not as a problem it proposes to teach us to live with. That it also serves the latter purpose is an incidental effect, not the conscious aim of any Zionism that truly faces the Exile And young men and women who, in the future, will turn with passion and eagerness to Zionism, whether secular or religious, will as in the past be those to whom the Exile presents itself as a personal problem that must be solved; who cannot take seriously the compromises American Jews are compelled to devise in order to live with it.

Herzl thought of Zionism as a positive solution for those who could not be assimilated or would not accept assimilation. His only alternative to Zionism was assimilation, for he thought of the Jewish problem almost exclusively as a problem to be solved. The situation today forces us to see the problem as one which large portions of Jewry, for years to come, must still seek not to solve but to live with. But where a possible solution exists, there will always be some —those who are least able to compromise—who will eagerly avail themselves of it.

The great sifting of the Jewish people upon which we embarked following the establishment of the State of Israel is a slower, subtler process than we could have foreseen. But it is still the cardinal event in our present Jewish era, the great key to the understanding of our times.

Postscript, 1983
Reconsiderations and
Amplification

T HIS ESSAY WAS
assembled and written in 1955, at the peak of the complacent
Eisenhower era, amid the self-satisfied celebrations of American Jewry. It was a restatement of Zionist assumptions that
spoke to that moment, but was not significantly affected by it.
The views set forth had been developed during the social upheavals of the 1930s and the total war of the 1940s, and they
responded to the trauma of the Holocaust and the revolutionary implications of the rise of Israel. It concluded with a prog-
nosis of the American Jewish situation, intended to apply well
beyond its time.

Nevertheless, it *was* written in the 1950s—an era generally regarded today as a long-outlived irrelevancy, a day
mired down in mindless platitudes and now completely sub-
merged by the "greening" of the 1960s. After the revolution
in life-styles and values by an intervening generation of rebels, anything written back then seems obviously to need re-
consideration. Consequently, the first task of this postscript
will be to reconsider prognoses formulated a quarter of a
century ago.

Some of the criticism of this essay by perceptive readers
pointed out problems clearly implied in my position, but not
dealt with explicitly. If I consider a consciousness of Exile the
essential element that gives meaning to Diaspora Jewish life,
and if I insist that "Exile" is a meta-historical concept, am I not
conceding that only religion can sustain and justify Jewish existence? On what grounds can I then continue to define myself
as a secularist Jew? To give a fuller account of this matter is the
second task of this postscript.

160]

The essay presented what I called a "Zionist analysis" of the two main elements of the modern Jewish problem, anti-Semitism and assimilation. In its classic presentations, Zionism (like its anti-Zionist opponents) promised to eliminate both problems in its own way. The "Zionist analysis" I offered expected that in neither case would this happen.

In contrast to their liberal opponents, Zionists saw anti-Jewish attitudes as a basic, not an accidental, feature of Jewish life in the Diaspora. But they hoped for the gradual disappearance of anti-Semitism—not through the spread of enlightenment (as non-Zionists did), but through the concentration of Jews in their homeland and the thinning out or eventual dissolution of the Diaspora. The same process was expected to remove the threat to Jewish survival from assimilation. A Jewish state would either assemble the bulk of Jewry in its own land, enabling the rest to become assimilated among the Gentiles; or alternatively would serve as a cultural center whose radiating influence would preserve the Diaspora Jews from assimilation.

My own analysis considered all these forecasts as highly improbable—dependent on extreme conditions that were unpalatable, as well as unlikely. I assumed that both anti-Semitism and the problems of Diaspora Jewry would survive the creation of Israel. In the years that have passed, however, some observers were led to believe that current conditions made the imminent disappearance of anti-Semitism more than likely; or that American Jewry was about to disappear by assimilation; or that a religious revival was transforming American Jewry into a center of independent, creative Jewish culture.

Anti-Semitism Reconsidered

As to anti-Semitism, the American Jewish Committee had been collecting public opinion polls on the subject since the 1930s, and as the 1950s drew to a close it undertook to summarize the findings and reexamine their significance. Twenty-five years of polling, collated and analyzed by the sociologist Charles H. Stember, were presented to a conference and subsequently published (together with the conference papers and discussions) in 1966—just as a new time of troubles in America was rising to high tide.[1]

Stember's analysis of the data found strong indications that European-style political anti-Semitism was about to disappear, once and for all, as a possible development in America. The standard indices of anti-Semitic feeling, after a rising trend in the 1930s and during the war (when Jews were held to be warmongers), had shrunk in some cases to insignificance, or declined to levels that inspired rosy predictions of future tranquility for American Jewry. In the discussion much comfort was taken from the lack of an anti-Semitic response to Israel's policy clashes with the U.S. government, or to the prominence of Jews in civil rights militancy, or even to the Rosenberg spy trial.

Other current trends seemed to some to provide a theory that justified extrapolating the apparent decline in anti-Semitic feeling into the indefinite future. American Jews of the 1960s, by now largely native-born, were moving out of the inner cities and "second-settlement" areas of their immigrant parents and grandparents into affluent suburbia and, as the magazines of the time reported, still more affluent and assimilated "exurbia." While suburban Jews remained socially segregated and clung together in tight communities, there were signs of a changing trend among the young. Jewish attendance at universities grew astoundingly, till four out of five college-age Jewish youths were soon enrolled; moreover, enrollments were heavily concentrated in the most highly reputed schools. Jewish representation on faculties leaped to impressive heights, as the bars of anti-Jewish discrimination were lowered after the war. And the new science-related industries offered this generation not only frontier opportunities; they gained young Jews acceptance in broader reaches of the economic, political, and social elite. All this might be questioned as being too close for comfort to the recent experience of German Jews: as being liable to arouse the hostility of Gentiles left behind in the competitive race. But it was pointed out in reply that the Jewish trend simply anticipated what America at large was also experiencing. The somewhat isolated eminence of the Jews would be overcome as other Americans became more "Jewish": better educated, more urban, better represented in service and professional jobs—and, in consequence, more tolerant.

What could be expected to emerge from all this remained rather vaguely stated. There was the specific prediction that

European-style political anti-Semitism was no longer possible in America; and since no distinction of consequence was made between political anti-Semitism and garden-variety, diffusely popular anti-Semitism, there was the clear impression that anti-Semitism as such was about to disappear.

The analysis I proposed does distinguish between the conditions for the rise of basic anti-Semitism and those under which various expressions of anti-Semitism, up to its political form, arise.[2] If basic anti-Semitism is rooted in the opposition aroused by Judaism itself, then only the disappearance of a people exclusively identified with Judaism—as the Jews are—could cause it to disappear. On the other hand, the politicization of anti-Semitism has its roots in the particular national history of any country where it takes effect.

Given these assumptions, one could not accept an interpretation of the data that made the postwar decline of *political* anti-Semitism appear to be the result of an apparent decline in *basic* anti-Semitism as well as a portent of the disappearance of both. It seemed far more likely that the changing political perception of the Jews (particularly the guilty sense of having abandoned them to the Nazi practice of genocide) explained the declining indices of anti-Jewish basic attitudes rather than vice versa. And if this was so, the interpretation of these data would have to be different: what they measured was simply a decline in the *respectability* of stereotypes associated with the Nazis. Respondents sensitized to the extreme connotations of certain questions simply avoided giving positive answers to them; but this was no reliable indicator of a decisive change in the permanent, cumulative, continually self-transforming complex of traditional attitudes towards the Jews in Gentile culture.

These views were soon confirmed, by research as well as by events. Another Jewish agency had sponsored a series of studies that focused on the anti-Semitic impact of religious beliefs (an aspect somewhat neglected in Stember's materials); these studies found basic anti-Semitism to persist with "tenacity."[3] The unrest of the mid-1960s released, among other passions, a varied range of anti-Semitic expressions as well. Since then, hardly anyone has assumed that anti-Semitism, basic or political, is following a steady curve of decline. Indeed, observers who have been following events as they occur in the

1980s seem generally to sense a rising level of anti-Semitic intensity—whether polls support this conclusion or not.

Also, the hypothesis that the name "anti-Semite" has become disreputable, but that the phenomenon itself survives under other names, has by now become a commonplace. The tactic of declaring themselves merely "anti-Zionists," while borrowing freely from the Protocols of the Elders of Zion, was adopted early by Arab spokesmen at the U.N. and elsewhere— at first with little success. But the anti-Semitic agitation of black nationalists in America during the 1960s, even when it dispensed with verbal masks, was perceived as simply black rage against white oppression, not anti-Semitism at all.[4] Over the years, this perception lent a growing legitimacy to anti-Semitic slogans—not to say attitudes—when they were presented as merely anti-Zionist. Instead of the shame that had inhibited the resort to hostile stereotypes, resentment against a sense of Gentile guilt that gave Jews political advantages was released in such expressions as De Gaulle's recuperation of ancient prejudice in November 1967, and with increasing freedom by others since then. Adding to the public acceptance of this hostility was the emergence, as a major Third World force, of peoples of non-Western civilizations who have no historic bonds with the Judaic tradition, whether for good or for ill. They have no reason to treat Israel, or the Jewish people, as anything more than another small nation or tribe: that is, quite amorally, and strictly in line with *raison d'état*. They can use or support anti-Semitism without feeling it.

On the other hand, the correct perception that code words can veil anti-Semitism (or other forms of prejudice and hostility) has become so popular a cliché that one must guard oneself against its abuse. The demagogic invocation of automatic Jewish responses to the cry of "anti-Semitism" by certain contemporary political leaders makes the need to do so painfully clear—especially when one considers what is involved in a Zionist analysis of anti-Semitism.

A Zionist analysis, as already noted, assumes anti-Semitism to be a basic, and not an accidental, feature of Jewish life—at least, in the Diaspora. It follows that, at least in the Diaspora, the problem cannot be eliminated; consequently, the early Zionists regarded attempts to combat anti-Semitism (a main concern of the established Jewish community) as useless, or merely palliative. Also, Herzl and other Zionists scandalized many, including their followers, by choosing to deal with what they considered to be rational aspects of certain anti-Semites' hostility to Jews: they assumed that both the Jews and their enemies had a common interest in removing densely settled Jews from Diaspora countries to a homeland of their own, and that an agreement to cooperate in achieving this goal could be negotiated.

This, of course, is only a partial account of any Zionist position on anti-Semitism and anti-Semites. Other, more deeply rooted and more emotional attitudes were always present, and were reinforced repeatedly by the blows of history. The first clearly Zionist impulse was one of rebellion and revulsion against Jewish helplessness (and above all, passivity) in the face of violent persecution, pogroms, and daily humiliation. This was certainly Herzl's primal Zionist impulse as well, notwithstanding his ability to set emotion aside and deal with anti-Semites. Other Zionists might agree that only by building a Jewish national home could anti-Semitism be overcome (which meant that "combatting" it in the Diaspora was futile), but could not stomach any dealings with enemies who made bloody war, or its moral equivalent, on the Jews. Still others (and this attitude prevailed after the turn of the twentieth century) held it a Zionist duty to resist and oppose anti-Semites actively at every moment and in every situation. As Zionists they did not expect that such political activism (if possible, in alliance with liberal or radical friends) would solve the Jewish problem or eliminate anti-Semitism. But since the first principle of Zionism was Jewish self-respect, or pride, open resistance to those who viciously offended it was an unconditional Zionist duty. A Zionist attitude like this ruled out any relationship with anti-Semites other than one of total opposition and rejection.[5]

All these variations implied that with the restoration of the Jews to independence in their own homeland the problem of anti-Semitism would vanish, and so would the issue of a proper relation to anti-Semites. Such an escape hatch is not available for an analysis like mine, tying anti-Semitism as it does to the very foundation of the history of Jewish existence. Even if one does not accept such an analysis, it is clear that in fact the rise of Israel did not spell the end of anti-Semitism—for whatever reason: whether because the ingathering is incomplete, or because the legitimate existence of Israel is still contested, or because Jewish homelessness is not, in fact, the sufficient cause of anti-Semitism. How to respond to anti-Semitism and anti-Semites thus remains an open issue. In order to deal with it properly, it is necessary to note certain distinctions.[6]

Basic anti-Semitism, generated by the inherent opposition between Judaism and other religious cultures, is an irreducible, minimal hostility that persists so long as recognizable Jews and Gentiles live together. But if Jews and Gentiles do live together, there must be an irreducible, minimal level of mutal tolerance as well. Anti-Semitism and tolerance are the two inseparable ingredients that together make up the Gentile side of the Jew-Gentile symbiosis. They combine in inverse proportions, but each element is part of a single, highly complex, ever-changing tradition that is universally present throughout the range of variance of the Jew-Gentile relationship.

This makes it difficult, of course, to single out those who are properly called anti-Semites. If even the tolerant Gentile shares some anti-Semitic perceptions and attitudes, then the mere listing of such attitudes held by any given person does not suffice to prove him an anti-Semite. One would have to show that anti-Semitic hostility is a dominant, salient, or central part of his attitudes. The distinction is a quantitative one—and therefore relative. The same is true in the matter of judging policies or particular actions to be anti-Semitic. A quantitative measure for tolerant actions toward Jews could not be the total absence of hostility to Jewishness (that could define "philo-Semitism," perhaps). A level of hostility not exceeding the conventional reservations regarding Jewishness, acceded to by Jews as well as Gentiles in the unspoken social consensus basic to their symbiosis, may be called tolerant. Similarly, an anti-Semitic policy or action need not be one that refuses to tolerate Jews on any terms (that might define a genocidal mania, perhaps), but one that is unwilling to accept the level at which, in the given society, Jews are tolerated. Who, or what, is considered either tolerant or anti-Semitic, then, is relative to the status conventionally granted at a given time or place.

How a Jew should deal with an anti-Semite is a question of style or etiquette in personal relations, not primarily of ideology. A clear distinction between ideologies may be made only in regard to the response to systematic anti-Semitic acts or policies. Zionism differs from any other Jewish stance in not responding automatically, as a simple matter of resisting or outwitting anti-Semites, to any attempt to undermine achieved Jewish status. Such an attempt is, of course, anti-Semitic by definition; but a Zionist may find the Jewish position in question to be of no benefit, or plainly harmful to the interest of Jews themselves, in a long, national perspective—in which case it becomes less important to answer anti-Semites in the manner they deserve than to resolve a situation in the way larger Jewish interests demand. But while Zionism, as a political system, may recommend this approach, not all Zionists, or even most of them, are ruled by such analysis. More usually they react on their impulses as Jews, like others.

Jewish national independence in Israel is a new status Jews have attained by the assent of an international consensus, and attempts to revoke or undermine such a status are naturally perceived as anti-Semtiic. But there are good reasons for connecting the Jewish restoration represented by a sovereign Israel with the basic, irreducible antagonism between Jews and Gentiles who have a stake in the Holy Land. That is one cause for the reluctant and insecure recognition the Jewish State has received, even after so many years. For the Muslim Arabs the culture shock of the emergence of the Jews as rulers in part of the Islamic domain is compounded by other grievances, territorial and political, particularly afflicting the Palestinian Arabs. If they seek on these grounds to revoke Israeli independence (an objectively anti-Semitic act that would destroy an equal status Jews have been accorded), it then becomes a delicate matter of judgment whether to respond politically, in terms of Jewish national interest, or impulsively, as a Jew would respond to an anti-Semite's flagrant assault on the central core of Jewish pride.

For American Jews the complex of emotions that ties together a sovereign Israel, able to defend itself, with the Holocaust, as well as with our own self-image, has made solidarity with the Jewish State an overwhelming, nearly universal impulse. Like other Jews, even those American Zionists who are most attuned to political calculation find themselves little inclined to weigh coolly Jewish national interests before reacting to the unbridled attacks Israel suffers regularly, or to Israeli retaliation.

In Israel, however, the realization of Zionist aims has had its effect. It has not, of course, cut off basic anti-Semitism at its roots; but it has immensely enhanced the proclivity to consider rationally national interests in disputes between Jews and others—including those that raise issues concerning an achieved Jewish status. Many African states who support barely veiled anti-Semitic resolutions in the U.N., with unabashed and cynical self-interest, are welcomed by the Israelis in the aid programs still being conducted for African trainees in Tel Aviv. The Israeli public includes many Zionists who are acutely aware of the demagogy at work when the spectre of anti-Semitism is used by Israeli leaders in order to confuse judgment, in situations where sound Zionist analysis would dictate a different approach: namely, to treat it as a mere tactical diversion when Israel's foes see fit to employ anti-Semitic demagogy for their purposes, and to concentrate on practical compromises that might be discussed—as in the end the Israelis and Arabs, without other option, have always done.

Assimilation Reconsidered

Some of the conclusions formulated in the 1950s concerning American Jewish assimilation involve assumptions that may be, or have been, questioned in the light of subsequent events. This applies to the following theses: that American Jews are an unassimilable minority because of a firm, religiously-based barrier; that a secular Jewishness would perforce continue, but had no meaningful future as a program for American Jews; and that American Judaism, lacking deep roots in living Jewish culture and reduced to a conventional cult, would generate successive cohorts of discontented young and sensitive Jews, uneasy with the established forms of Jewish identification and open to diverse alternatives.

To speak of American Jews as an "unassimilable minority," was more plausible in the 1950s than it is now, because it was the generally accepted estimate at that time that no more than 10% of marriages involving Jews were intermarriages with Gentiles. This meant that all but a small fringe of American

168]

Jewry were exposed only to the public face of Christian civilization, not having intimate family relations with Gentiles. Even at that time it was clear that existing dating patterns of college-age Jews might change this radically very soon.[7] Indeed, shortly afterwards studies began to show intermarriage rates in the younger generation at the level of pre-Hitler Germany: up to 40 percent of marriages involving Jews, in some studies, were found to be with Gentile partners.

There was an immediate outcry that the threat of biological submergence once foreseen by statisticians for German Jewry was now to be feared in America. Intermarriage, a low birthrate, and assimilation could thin out the ranks of Jewry and erase all traces of the community within the space of a few generations. But it was evident that such predictions were manifestations of panic, not realistic analysis: one could reject on principle, for a start, predictions that extrapolated without limit the trend of the moment. There was no reason to think that a substantial Jewish population would not remain untouched by intermarriage: even in the study that showed two out of five marriages involving Jews to be intermarriages, six out of the eight young Jews involved were getting married to other Jews. Demographers applied their usual hairsplitting finesse to the latest data and a lively debate soon broke out as to whether the religious conversions that accompanied intermarriage were causing the Jewish community to lose or gain in the statistical balance sheet.

Whatever the net demographic effect of intermarriage may be, two things are certain: First, intermarriage itself is not an automatic "structural" assimilation. This final step is still dependent on a religious conversion—and that can go either way. Second, intermarriage is an additional element (and, in principle, one of critical significance) complicating the already tortuous problem of defining an adequate, meaningful identity for many American Jews. Whatever happens in the nuclear family (and despite the loss in cohesion of the modern extended family), the spread of intermarriage has put many in the position of straddling the old Jew-Gentile division, making identification with either side, with neither, or vaguely with both, conceivable options for the children of such unions. For a parallel one would have to look to the prewar Central European Jewries, or to the ex-Marrano Jews of the past.

The potential for assimilation into Gentile society, through entry into the Christian communion, is heightened by this development, of course. So, too, the passage into Judaism from the outside has been made easier; and despite the oft-noted greater enthusiasm for their newly-acquired Judaism shown by converted, compared with their Jewish-born, spouses, one effect has been to attach to the community a fringe element with an awareness of the style of Jewish culture and a sense of its values that may be even less developed than that of the average passive and indifferent American Jew. Rather than solving the Jewish problem by speeding assimilation, the rise in intermarriage may have swelled the ranks—of some synagogues, but also of the Jews-in-name-only; and that has helped make more acute, as well as more obscure, the problem of a meaningful Jewish identity.

By 1982, doubts long voiced—and long stoutly denied—about the prospects of Jewish secular culture in America (by which, conceivably, unsynagogued Jews as well as others might be meaningfully integrated ethnically) have become virtual certainties. The Yiddish press that still fought for its existence in the 1950s has almost vanished, together with most of its supporting infrastructure. The devoted efforts of loyal champions to find a place for Yiddish in the curriculum of universities and public schools amount, under the circumstances, to a concession that it has become a cult rather than the voice of a living culture.

Yet for a while in the 1960s there were those who preached the revival of ethnic, secular Jewishness in America.[8] They hoped to entrench it in public, institutional forms such as would have gladdened the heart of Mordecai M. Kaplan and honored the memories of Ahad Ha'am and Simon Dubnow. Blacks, Hispanics, and American Indians were successfully making claims, as "minorities," for the preservation under public law of their ethnic heritage, as well as for the advancement of their social-economic status. Some young Jews urged their community to join this trend and bolster the American Jewish ethnic identity in the same way. But events soon destroyed the illusory hope they shared.

It was not only that the certified "minorities" (as well as government agencies) rejected Jews as a possible "minority," even while granting this status to homosexuals and women as qualified groups; nor was it simply that the Jewish establishment (apart from a few old Zionists who saw "affirmative action" as something cognate to their claims for Jews in Palestine) preferred to rely on individual, not collective, rights, and on "meritocracy." The ground on which a claim to "minority" status must now stand in order to be recognized is a current history of social and economic underprivilege—so that the majority of the population, who are women, become a legitimate "minority." Given this prerequisite, one can effectively attach demands for preserving one's cultural heritage to an American "minority rights" agenda. Lacking it, the claim stands little chance of being heard.

Jews today are classed as part of the privileged majority in America. Any ethnic claims they might seek to advance politically would have to be based on cultural difference alone without social-economic grievances of consequence to back them up. If this had been seriously attempted during the recent revival of "ethnicism," it would have met the same official and popular incomprehension it had always encountered in America. A self-assertive Jewish ethnicism might find allies in the new climate of opinion, but in unfamiliar quarters. Orthodox American Jews may be compatible fellows, for limited purposes, in the ethnic backlash of second-generation Middle Americans—particularly, in regard to the pluralistic, parochial Catholic campaign for public support of their school system. But such allies would offer little or no assistance to any conceivable program for the revival of secular Jewishness in the United States.

The outbreak of cultism during the "greening" of America could hardly have been foreseen in the 1950s, in spite of the "beatniks" of that time, who have since become countercultural culture-heroes. Nevertheless, the analysis of the Jewish situation then formulated sufficiently indicated conditions that fostered the disproportionate Jewish share in the subsequent cultist wave, in all its forms. Briefly, this essay had concluded that a religiously oriented, highly Americanized neo-Zionism was most likely to dominate the community consensus in the foreseeable future. It also expected that such a "civic religion" of American Jewry would fail to deal adequately with the identity problems of its younger and more sensitive members—

problems made more salient precisely because the religious public image of the community implied that the contemporary synagogue offered emotionally persuasive and intellectually cogent answers to questions of ultimate belief. But the traditional Jewish religion tended to avoid elaborate dogmatic rationalization—and its prime symbolic interpreter of both cosmic and human history was the "meta-myth" of Exile and Redemption, which the American Jewish establishment so regularly downplays. The Americanized synagogue offers no comparable meaningful experience, whether intellectual or aesthetic, that could firmly anchor a drifting Jewish identity; wherefore the attractions of cultism are not surprising.

In the flight from the conformity of the synagogues, Jewish cultist enthusiasts have either taken up a wide range of minor movements, theosophical and political, or simply adopted the counterculture of self-indulgence or self-destruction—all far removed from anything within the range of an authentic Jewish style. But others, moved by similar impulses of rebellion, sought their liberation within their own religion, renovating, reconstructing, or reforming its tradition in line with one version or another of the new taste. This development has been hailed as the renewal of a creative Jewish tradition in the Diaspora; and some claim it places American Jewry on a par with Israel, or above it, as a prime, independent source of the authentic Jewish culture of the future.

Those familiar with the favorite Jewish writers and thinkers of the new trend will find outdated the intellectual opposition this essay chose to confront. In the 1950s it was natural to assume that the Conservative rabbinate—especially that section under Mordecai Kaplan's influence—was the most representative intellectual voice of the community, and most decisively articulated its institutional principles. Even then, of course, Conservative rabbinical students were more likely to be moved by Abraham Joshua Heschel's mystical neo-Hassidism than by Kaplan. Today, if one were to take on those ideologues and thinkers who are the leading intellectual lights of religiously committed Jewish youth, one would choose German figures like Rosenzweig, Buber, or Scholem, and their local disciples—or the Orthodox philosopher Rabbi Joseph Soloveichik—rather than the Reconstructionist school of American Jewish Pragmatism built by Kaplan.

172]

This intellectual fashion certainly mirrors the unrest of those who seek more explicit theological comfort than the Americanized synagogue cares to provide. The mode of thinking (notwithstanding Buber's stress on the interpersonal nature of human existence) is highly subjective and inward-directed compared to the outward-looking, communally-oriented style of the Kaplan school. It is true that American Jewry has been enriched, by the rebellions of men now in their forties and fifties, with important new institutions: the *havurah* fellowships or conventicles; the Hebrew day schools; the spread of Judaic studies into the general universities. But it is striking that the new tools for survival serve the community's cultic needs: education; the nurture of piety within a more protective, intimate social milieu; and the preservation and elucidation of the past. They do not, like Kaplan's valiant attempts to reconstruct an "organic community," face seriously the issue of what is needed in order to make good the claim to preserve a living, authentic *culture* of Jewishness in America. The whole style (even apart from the continued, embarrassed suppression of a sense of Exile) is plainly that of a cult.

On the question of authenticity, it should be noted that the currently revived Jewish religious fashion is not only a derivative, but a doubly derivative phenomenon. It is clear that the local, characteristically Jewish experience—that of the synagogue, primarily—cannot adequately nourish a living Jewish culture, if cultivated American Jews have to seek in the nostalgic past and in other Jewries the thought, and the myth-sustaining history, that could make their Jewishness meaningful. To sustain themselves as Jews in America, devotees may build on Buber and neo-Hassidism, on Rosenzweig or Rabbi Kook, or even on the Yiddishist cult of the onetime Jewish labor Bund in Poland. But all of these (with the telling exception of the ill-fated Bund) were derivative themselves, not authentic outgrowths of their local situation: Buber and Rosenzweig drew on the life of prewar Eastern Europe, not on their own German milieu; and Rabbi Kook painted a Messianic, religious, futuristic vision of what the life of contemporary, secularist Zionist workers might mean ultimately in religious terms. These are sources from which Jewish intellectuals may find palliative relief, but they hold little promise for implanting an authentic, living Jewish culture in America.

Religious dedication may sustain a cult. An authentic, living culture depends on confronting the serious secular problems of a society, its full immediate experience, in the light of its historic tradition, conveyed and mediated in its own style. This kind of a situation exists for Jews only in Israel today.

Amplification: Jewish Secularism

The idea of a secular Jewish identity, national but not religious, has had a natural appeal for many Jews who are detached from the synagogue but not from their Jewishness. In common with the secular nationalism of other peoples, Jewish secularism in principle disregards religious belief as a criterion of national identity. This is a divorce that is particularly hard to carry out consistently in the Jewish case. A Jew who is only nominally, or not at all, committed to Jewish religious beliefs and practices may be universally treated as a Jew, by Gentiles, by other Jews, and by traditional Jewish law. But a man who claims to be a Jew by nationality, though converted to another religion, has been ruled to be no Jew by the secular courts of Israel, relying on the consensus that the tribunal found to prevail in social conventions; and the contrary view of traditional law failed to sway the assenting opinion even of the Orthodox themselves. In the first case, Jewishness has been divorced from religious belief; in the second, it has not.

A similar inconsistency has been claimed by critics, as noted earlier, when I say that "Exile," explicitly defined as meta-historical, is the idea that makes sense of Jewish history to this day, so that without a sense of Exile Jewish experience loses its meaning.[9] Yet I not only note the difficulties that the Holocaust and Israel's rise present for the traditional idea, but claim to be speaking as a Jewish secularist in defending it. It is necessary to make clear the grounds for this, no doubt, paradoxical position by considering the nature of Jewish secularism.

Secularist nationalism has developed along different lines among different peoples; but one may say that there is a classic pattern represented by the history of nationalism in Western Europe. The defense of local religious traditions and interests against foreign domination was a factor in the early history, or prehistory, of nationalism, to be sure. But the most significant pattern was the liberation of significant institutions from the control of the universal church. Language and literature, no longer confined to church Latin as the sole medium for high culture, flourished in an efflorescence of national secular traditions. Music and art emerged from the cloisters and courts in an enthusiastic cultivation of the riches of folk lore. And of course politics and history were taken over as the primary domain of national sovereignties.

In this general devolution from ecumenical and imperial to local, national control, two significant spheres nevertheless remained universal aspects of a single European civilization, transcending national frontiers. One was the humanist culture and experimental science of the new modernity, upon which was based the common technical civilization of the West. The other was the Christian tradition common to the European nations, providing a common style of communication that allowed all to maintain a basic level of civility and seek a common ground in conscience in their dealings with one another.

The new era announced by the eighteenth-century Enlightenment and the emancipation it inspired meant to many Jews the hope that they could find not merely toleration but equality and fraternity in the new nations. A national culture freed from the church, they thought, was one they could share; especially since Judaism, an ideological and book culture, had always been open to local variants in aesthetic matters, assigned by tradition to the Gentiles as their sphere. It was even easier to accommodate to the humanistic science, not to speak of the inherently neutral technology, basic to Western civilization. Jews could claim (and did) that their own religion was essentially identical with the deistic "scientific" rationalism assumed to be a moral foundation shared by all modern nations and common in principle to all mankind.

It turned out, of course, that the common ethos of the Europeans was rooted far less in humanism or science (these were the common culture of an international intellectual elite) than in the Christian heritage of the West. Christians of different nations and of rival sects and denominations, and even atheists reared as Christians, shared a vocabulary of values and a calendar of legends by which they knew each other to be akin; and in this universal European code, the Jews were known to be outsiders, the black sheep thrust out of the fold.[10]

Nothing has proved harder for modern Jews to accept than this, the truth they feel in their bones. There is, indeed, so much common ground between Judaism and Christianity (or Islam), in terms of ethical precepts and models, ultimate metaphysical assumptions, and the origins of ritual ideas, that in an era of growing ecumenicism there is much to unite them. What divides—a quarrel over legitimacy, birthright, and the proper exegesis of texts, many of which are jointly venerated—all this, to an uninvolved secular eye, may seem like pointless quibbling. (And yet to the same eye it may seem much less puzzling that Trotskyites and Stalinists, for example, had murderous quarrels over much the same kind of issue of legitimate succession in Marxism.) Nevertheless, it is these matters—questions of historical style and form, rather than matters of timeless substance—that separate the Jews from the several Gentile worlds. The separation applies with no less force to the unbelievers who, in the degree of their Jewishness, share an historical style and perspective at odds with the world of the Gentiles, or at least are not attuned by birth and breeding to the native perspectives of their unbelieving Gentile comrades.

Hence, when the Jews appropriated for their own purposes the idea of a secular nationalism, they found their situation to differ radically from the model they aspired to reproduce. They might cultivate a secular Hebrew or Yiddish literature, build a new Yiddish folk-theater, musical style, and freshly created painterly tradition; they might reclaim an active political role through Zionism and the Jewish labor movement, and rewrite Jewish history as an epic of embattled nationality. They might take an honored place in the brotherhood of humanist science. But what they could not do was to find their place in the brotherhood of European nations joined in the ethos of a common (Occidental) Christian civilization.

A similar outcome, to be sure, was not unknown in other cases. An element of conscious opposition to the European West, rooted obscurely in the clash of Occidental and Eastern Christianity, is an integral part of the history of Slavophil nationalism; and the nations of the Far East and of Islam have always distinguished between Western technical civilization and Western spiritual culture, making the defense of their own religious tradition against the inroads of Westernism part of their nationalist ideal. But there is a cardinal difference between all these cases and the Jewish predicament. All the others, like Occidental Christianity, are expressions of great religious civilizations, encompassing a number of different nations. The nationalism of each unit of such a civilization shares with others, in its oppostion to the Occident, the brotherhood of a common ethos, a transnational world-historical perspective. The Jews alone stand alone. The consequences of this unsought isolation are felt by secular nationalists and other Jewish secularists, both in Israel and the Diaspora, in different ways.

Israel as a Jewish nation ("as Jewish as Britain is British," to use Weizmann's old formula) expresses itself not only through its own language, politics, sense of making history, and other local, particularistic, folk activities such as all nations display to the world. It also finds itself related in an unparalleled way to an historical ethos not shared with any other people. This ethos becomes part of Israeli nationalism in a way unlike the typical relation of Western secular nationalists to their Christian heritage, or to other merely historical parts of their identity.

A Frenchman may take the same detached—somewhat humorous, somewhat appreciative—and essentially aesthetic attitude to the religious infatuation of one of his Crusader forefathers as might an Englishman, let us say, to the piratical career of one of his freebooter ancestors, or a wealthy American liberal to the political corruption and financial skullduggery once practiced by the long-dead founder of his family fortune. But a founding father of Israel socialism (in a moral example subsequently echoed by one of his prominent successors) asks, How can one teach Israeli children to understand their ancestors' horror and panic when the Romans defiled the Temple walls with swine, if Israelis today raise pigs in the Holy Land? The excessive influence conceded to the Orthodox political parties (by an electorate that is mainly secular in its beliefs and practices) is not merely the result of political calculations concerning workable government coalitions; it is also rooted in this sense of the vital national function of the religious culture exclusively possessed by Israel. The same sense has much to do with the turn toward religion by younger Israelis reared on secular principles by socialist parents. And it has a pervasive influence of a different kind on those Jewish secularists in Israel who cannot bring themselves to accept a religious commitment simply because of their national or other extraneous concerns. They grow up in a society, and through the medium of a language, in which the Jewish historical ethos is the original, all-pervasive matrix of value-symbols that shapes their perception of everything that happens. All their serious social, political, and economic problems happen to them as Jews. As secularists they are free to use, or ignore, such parts of their heritage as their whim may dictate; and sheer ignorance may leave much of the more profound deposits of historic Hebrew culture beyond their grasp and possible use. But potentially it is all available to them, in the measure of their Hebrew literacy; and the actual vicissitudes of their lives compel them to draw on the resources of their Jewishness continually. In this way they nourish the renewed growth of authentic Jewish culture.

The situation of Diaspora Jews is in some ways similar, but differs in critical respects. The exclusive Jewish relation to a unique historical ethos, and the isolation it entails, applies to the Diaspora as well as to Israel. But not since the dense, autonomous Jewish settlements of earlier times and other places were dissolved, and the sense of a palpable Exile was suppressed or dissipated, has the Jewish ethos been a living culture in the Diaspora. Some cling to a Jewish cult, shaping it often to their convenience or capacity to believe. For others, including a major part of Jewish secularists, their Jewishness is largely negative, a matter of naked isolation. It does not enfold them with the warmth and steady force of a comprehensive environment—but it does preclude them from a natural (rather than cultist) identification with the Gentile environment that constantly presses upon them. Because of their Jewishness they are isolated; and because they are not Israelis, their isolation is individual rather than communal.

There are several ways to cope with the discomfort this situation may produce. Some of the possible resolutions are clearly mere fictions. This is notably the case with the old claim that to be "alienated"—that is, to be an isolated, free-floating individual—is to be not only a higher type of man, but a quintessential Jew. As a doctrine of normative Jewishness, this is only one, and far from the most appealing, of many rational-izations that seek to hypostatize some convenient aspect of the Jewish historical experience as its enduring essence: for in-stance, statelessness, landlessness, or the perpetual awaiting of the never-to-be-really-expected Messiah. If isolation is taken as a maxim used to guide personal behavior, it discredits itself continually, as the apostles of alienation cluster in fictive com-munities of the disinherited; such communities serve only as temporary shelters for a lost generation, but with no historic viability. Only by resort to cultism (Jewish or not) is Jewish isolation in the Diaspora capable of being made communal, not individual; but this is to renounce either secularism or Jewish-ness, or both together.

Another escape hatch for the isolated Jewish secularist is to reduce the whole issue of Jewishness to a triviality, not part of the serious concerns of a secular American Jew. Many adopt this expedient; and they are not far removed in spirit from those Jews who use an occasional visit to the synagogue, or a Jewish lodge or country club, as the total expression of their Jewishness.

Jewish isolation is neither a triviality nor a condition of individual maladjustment. Its roots are deeply imbedded in his-tory and extend to a communal experience of great age and wide variety. The isolation of the secular Jew, in the Diaspora no less than in Israel, derives from that history and experience; and the myth-image by which the Jewish ethos has made their mean-ing concrete for successive generations has been the linked sym-bol-set of Exile and Redemption. Secularists cannot be expected to hold sacred each letter of the liturgy by which the community periodically celebrates its myth; nor do many traditionalist Jews. But there is a necessary movement in the progress of the self-un-derstanding of a secular (or, for that matter, cult-affiliated) Dias-pora Jew. That self-understanding must go beyond the mere perception of personal isolation or the simple positive identifica-tion with one's immediate communal source, one's own Diaspora community. True self-understanding requires a full openness to the Jewish communal experience everywhere and at all times, and to its continued creative unfolding—most authentically in Israel and, under the age-old, protean imagery of Exile, wher-ever Jews still live with the consciousness of their unique histori-cal ethos.

NOTES

AMERICA IS DIFFERENT

1 Cited in C. Bezalel Sherman's article, "Nationalism, Secularism and
Religion in the Jewish Labor Movement," *Judaism*, Fall 1954 (Tercentenary
Issue), p. 355. The statement occurs in a manifesto issued by "Abraham
Cahan, Organizer," on behalf of the Hebrew Federation of Labor of the
United States and Canada, which was published in *Die Arbeiter Zeitung*
(New York), December 5, 1890, two months after the Federation's founding
convention. The full text is reproduced in E. Tcherikower's *Geshikhte fun
der Yidisher arbeter-bavegung in die Fareynikte Shtatn* (New York, 1945),
Vol. II, pp. 499-502.

2 When American anti-Semites avail themselves of election periods in order
to conduct their propaganda, they do, of course, formulate "programs."
The provisions relating to Jews in these documents are usually more
vituperative than programmatic in character, and they combine obvious,
though rather feeble, imitation of European models with some specific
American features, reflecting animosity against American Jewish organizations.
I owe the following typical examples to the courtesy of my friend Jack
Baker of the Anti-Defamation League: In William Dudley Pelley's (The
Silver Shirt) Weekly, on September 5, 1934, appeared "The New Emancipation Proclamation—The Silver Shirt Program." It proposed "racial quotas
on the political and economic structure" in order to prevent Jewish office-
holding "in excess of the ratio of (Jews) ... in the body politic." All Jews,
and all foreign-born persons not "completely naturalized," were to be
registered, under severe penalties for evasion. All Jews were to be compelled
to "forswear forever ... Jewish allegiance," and any Jew apprehended in
giving support to Jewish nationalism was to be criminally prosecuted for
sedition. (Quoted in Gustavus Myers, *History of Bigotry in the United States*
[New York, 1943], pp. 405-6.)

The 1948 election platform of Gerald L. K. Smith's Christian Nationalist
Party called for "the immediate deportation of all supporters of the political
Zionist movement" and the outlawry of "this international machine and all
its activity." Such "Jewish Gestapo organizations" as "the so-called Anti-
Defamation League, the American Jewish Congress, the so-called Non-
Sectarian Anti-Nazi League, the self-styled Friends of Democracy" were
to be dissolved. Immigration of "Asiatics, including Jews, and members
of the colored races" was to be stopped. The partition of Palestine was
opposed. The party program published by Smith in 1952, however, had no
such specific references to Jews.

The nine point "Program of the National Renaissance Party" (published
in the National Renaissance *Bulletin*, October, 1953, pp. 3 and 4) proposed,
under point 1, to "repudiate the operetta-State of Israel;" in point 2, "to

enforce a strict policy of racial segregation in America;" and in point 3, "to bring about a gradual deportation of "unassimilable elements . . ." *viz.*, the "Porto Ricans, Negroes, Jews and Asiatics;" in point 4, to bar Jews "from all political and professional posts" and to forbid marriage between Jews and "members of the dominant White Race;" and in point 6, to base American foreign policy upon a "German-American alliance in Europe; a Moslem-American alliance in the Middle East; and a Japanese-American alliance in Asia" (Reproduced in the U.S. House of Representatives, Committee on Un-American Activities, *Preliminary Report on Neo-Fascist and Hate Groups*, Washington, Dec. 17, 1954, pp. 21-2).

See also Richard Hofstadter's comment on the tendency of the political attitudes of the "new American right" to express themselves "more in vindictiveness, in sour memories, in the search for scapegoats, than in realistic proposals for action" ("The Pseudo-Conservative Revolt" in *The New American Right,* Daniel Bell, ed. [New York, 1955], p. 44, and note similar observations in other sources referred to by Hofstadter (*Ibid.,* p. 54, note 7.)

[3] See Graetz's narrative of the "Synhedrion" in Paris and the events leading up to it, *History of the Jews* (Jewish Publication Society translation, Philadelphia, 1895), Vol. V, pp. 474-509.

[4] See Chapter II, note 9 below.

[5] David Shub (in *The Jewish Daily Forward,* New York, May 15, 1955) says that this sentiment was attributed by Zionists to the Jewish Socialist leader Vladimir Medem (1879-1923), and was always denied by Medem and his associates. Whatever the origin of the quotation, which I have not been able to check further, it became a popular byword succinctly expressing an attitude of which Russian and Polish Jews had had several striking evidences among revolutionaries.

A pamphlet inciting to pogroms was issued by the revolutionary *Narodnaya Volya* group, and though it was withdrawn subsequently, there was a continuing discussion of the advisability of using anti-Semitism to foster a revolutionary atmosphere. The shock effect of this event on the Russian Jewish *intelligentsia* is described in Abraham Liessin's "Episodes," in the Yiddish Scientific Institute's *Historishe Shriften,* Vol. III (Vilna-Paris, 1939), pp. 196-200. It was from this same time that we date the reaction of a significant group of Russian Jewish intellectuals against the ideal of Emancipation and the rise of the counter-ideal of Auto-Emancipation.

[6] See, however, Judd L. Teller's article, "America's Two Zionist Traditions," in *Commentary,* October, 1955, pp. 343-52. This article emphasizes the existence of a pre-Herzlian Zionist "tradition" in America, represented by Mordecai Emanuel Noah and Emma Lazarus. It also highlights the difference in attitude between some native-born (or American-educated) early Zionists, like Louis D. Brandeis and Julian W. Mack, and the Eastern European outlook of immigrant Zionism. In common with many writers during the recent Tercentenary celebrations of American Jewry, Teller strains the data perceptibly in an effort to make episodes add up to a native American Jewish tradition; but the differences he emphasizes between the Zionism of the immigrant ghetto and the Zionism of "Uptown" Jews is a significant one, in view of the similarity of the latter to the neo-Zionist mood of today. Illustrations of early "native American" Zionist views will be found in a source book on Zionist thought, *The Zionist Debate,* edited by Arthur Hertzberg, which is being prepared for publication.

Chapter II

THE AMERICAN JEWISH PROBLEM

1 Will Herberg, *Protestant-Catholic-Jew, An Essay in American Religious Sociology,* (New York, 1955), p. 53.

2 Concerning the character and development of the American "ecclesiastical polity," see H. Richard Niebuhr, *The Social Sources of Denominationalism* (New York, 1929), especially Chapters VI though IX.

3 As Yehezkel Kaufmann has so conclusively proved in his monumental Hebrew study, *Golah v'Nekhar* ("Exile and Alienhood"), the constitution and preservation over the centuries of the Jewish historic nationality is a consequence of the fact that (apart from insignificant episodes) Judaism never succeeded in converting other peoples than the Jews.

4 It is needless to consider at length the point that Sefardic, German, and East European Jews merged in America, for all Jewish group throughout the Diaspora have always had a common historic consciousness far more significant than their differences. Certainly the differences among various Jewish groups are something of which *Gentiles* usually remained unaware.

5 Of the Southern apologists for slavery, only John C. Calhoun is important as an influence on contemporary thought, through his criticism of unqualified majority rule. His defense of slavery is not, of course, of any current significance. Nor do other writers, such as George Fitzhugh, whose defense of slavery was central to his thought, figure anywhere but in textbooks or sourcebooks in the history of American social thought. The last to cite such "authorities" would certainly be the anti-Negro bigots of our times, who see little need of philosophy to back up their politics.

6 See Chapter I, pp. 17-20, and Chapter II, p. 48 ff., above.

7 See for a sketch of his brief and extraordinary life Theodor Lessing, *Der Juedische Selbsthass* (Berlin, 1930), pp. 80-100, or Felix A. Theilhaber, *Judenschicksal* (Tel Aviv, undated), pp. 151-75.

8 Paula Ceilson, "The Fortress," in *Integrity,* August, 1947, Vol. I, No. 11.

9 The same attempt to depreciate the differences between Jew and Christian may be noted in the cynical anecdotes related concerning a number of outstanding Jews who underwent baptism. There is a long repertoire of such stories, from Heine's remark that he acquired his baptismal certificate as a ticket of admission to European society to the quip of the famous Orientalist Chwolsohn that he was converted out of conviction—the conviction that it was better to be a professor in Petersburg than a *melamed* in Shnipishok.

In the urge to joke about their own conversion, one cannot fail to note the bad conscience of the authors about the renegadism implied in their "passing."

[10] See Chapter III, Notes 13 and 14 below

[11] On this whole development, see Yehezkel Kaufmann, *Golah v'Nekhar* (second printing, Tel Aviv, 1954), especially Vol. I, pp. 283-301.

[12] For a survey of this and related subjects see Nathan Glazer, "Social Characteristics of American Jews, 1654-1954," in the *American Jewish Year Book* 1955, pp. 3-41 (note especially pp. 25 ff. on the contemporary situation.)

[13] The reference is, of course, to the analysis developed in *The Lonely Crowd* (New Haven, 1950) by David Riesman, in collaboration with Reuel Denney and Nathan Glazer.

[14] See Eugen Rosenstock (-Hüssy), *Die Europäischen Revolutionen* (Jena, 1931) and *Out of Revolution* (New York, 1938), on these themes. Concerning the "calendar method" of historical philosophizing shared by Rosenstock and Franz Rosenzweig, see the Appendix, Franz Rosenzweig *Briefe* (Berlin, 1935) pp. 641 ff.

[15] This formulation is not original with the present writer, but is derived from a document. In a programmatic report issued in 1942 by a newly established "Commission on New Approaches to American Jewish Education," the following statement appears: "We soon agreed that there was great need for our children to be taught the fundamentals of the heritage which, willingly or unwillingly, was theirs; since, being Jews (by the age-old definition that the world would so regard them) it was better for them to be Jews and like it than to be Jews only by social compulsion."

Chapter III

SECULAR SOLUTIONS OF THE PROBLEM

1 Arthur Koestler, *Promise and Fulfillment* (New York, 1949), pp. 332-35. Some of the same themes (though inverted and subtly modulated) appear in the curiously inconclusive articles and addresses recently being composed by Isaiah Berlin on this subject. However, Mr. Berlin is far from committing himself to anything so decisive as assimilation. See his article "Jewish Slavery and Emancipation," in *Forum* (Jerusalem), December, 1953, pp. 52-68.

2 See Chapter II, pp. 48-54, 59-65, above.

3 In a more refined form, a similar idea was considered by Herzl only two years before he came to Zionism. He suggested that Jewish parents, without having to pretend for themselves a conversion which was not genuine, could solve the Jewish problem, if they would all baptize their children before the youngsters were old enough to exercise independent judgment. See the account in Herzl's diary, *Gesammelte Zionistische Werke* (Berlin, 1934, second printing), vol. II, pp. 7-10. A one-volume selection from Herzl's diaries, edited by Marvin Lowenthal and published by Dial Press, will be available in 1956. See also Koestler's *The Trail of the Dinosaur* (New York, 1955), pp. 106-41.

4 Mr. Milton Himmelfarb was kind enough to call my attention to a curious address delivered before the Rodeph Shalom (Philadelphia) Men's Club on May 15, 1948 by Rabbi Louis Wolsey. Rabbi Wolsey, a founder of the American Council for Judaism, Inc., explained that he had withdrawn from the Council because of "an influx of members who looked upon the Council as a device for assimilation, or for adventuring, or as a balm for those who did not believe in organized religion." Rabbi Louis Wolsey, *Sermons and Addresses* (Philadelphia, 1950), pp. 12-16. In contrast to such use of religion as no more than a mask for anti-Zionism, there is the characteristic case of the Boston rabbi, of an earlier period, who distilled his Judaism into such a pure and rational essence that he withdrew entirely from Judaism. See Arthur Mann, "Charles Fleischer's Religion of Democracy," *Commentary,* June, 1954, pp. 557-65. The most outstanding case of such a development is, of course, Felix Adler, founder of Ethical Culture.

5 Something of the kind may be observed in sects like Christian Science and, especially, Ethical Culture which have had a great attraction for marginal Jews.

6 It is not our contention, of course, that Soviet policy was aimed consistently and deliberately at assimilating the Jews. Neither the anti-

religious campaign nor the tendency to scatter the Jews geographically and occupationally had so definite or so specifically Jewish an objective.

7 This tendency, strikingly demonstrated in the history of the Jewish immigrants in America, is also illustrated by the social history of the Jewish settlement in Argentina. In this case the trend of Jews to the cities and to higher income occupations had to overcome an original planned concentration in farm colonies. The idea of scattering Jews geographically and socially in order to assimilate them is not, by the way, a pure abstraction. Such projects were mooted in French Revolutionary and Napoleonic times and attempted in the Austro-Hungarian and Russian Empires during periods of Enlightenment.

8 See references in Chapter I, note 6 above.

9 For a collection of his views on this subject and on Jewish questions generally, see Horace M. Kallen, *Judaism at Bay* (New York, 1932) , and *"Of Them Which Say They Are Jews" and Other Essays on the Jewish Struggle for Survival* (New York, 1954) .

10 Horace Kallen has suggested, at least, that ethnic experiences have really more profoundly influenced cultures than "universal" religions, that the universality of religions is only apparent and artificial. See Horace M. Kallen, *Judaism at Bay*, pp. 93-96. He has pointed out the particular character that religions acquire in different countries, and suggested that really Catholicism and Protestantism are different cultural entities in each country. The culmination toward which this view points is only suggested by Kallen but made very emphatically by Mordecai M. Kaplan: in its logical conclusion, this view holds that religion itself simply is the metaphysical form in which a collectivity expresses its historic cosmic experience. Each nation (not only the Jews!) would, accordingly, have its own proper religion. But this is going a great deal beyond the facts. The evidence shows rather that religion is a source of culture independent of ethnic experience; that the two may interweave in quite different ways; that among Christian peoples, the tendency to absorb religion entirely into a specific national form never reaches completion, but is always opposed by a tendency to revive a religious culture transcending ethnic difference—and making, incidentally, a far more serious and personal appeal to the ordinary individual.

11 See "Hebraism and Current Tendencies in Philosophy," *Ibid.*, pp. 7-15.

12 See, for example, *"Of Them Which Say They Are Jews,"* pp. 4-7, 35-41, 42-6, 59-60, 76f., 87-9, etc.

13 See, for an explicit articulation of this view, Paul Goodman, "The Judaism of a Man of Letters," *Commentary*, September, 1948, pp. 241-3. Similar themes are expressed in Harold Rosenberg, "The Herd of Independent Minds," *Ibid.*, pp. 244-52, and "Marc Chagall: Jewish Modernist Master," *Jewish Frontier*, April, 1945, pp. 26-33.

14 Most clearly in Daniel Bell, "A Parable of Alienation," *Jewish Frontier*, November, 1946, pp. 12-19. See also Irving Howe, "The Lost Young Intellectual," *Commentary*, October, 1946, pp. 361-7.

15 Waldo Frank, *The Jew in Our Day* (New York, 1944) , pp. 54-8, 74-8, 91-6, 174-86.

16 Speeches at the Zionist Congress and at sessions of the Zionist General Council by Dr. Samuel Margoshes, Mrs. Rose Halprin and other American Zionist leaders developed this theory with more or less clarity, in response to Israeli challenges.

17 For a representative statement, see the programmatic address delivered by Dr. Moshe Davis at the American Zionist Assembly on December 6, 1953. A short version is published in *The American Zionist*, January 5, 1954, pp. 9-12.

18 Nothing like a fixed "coefficient of tolerance" for difference exists, of course, but what is tolerated at one time in given conditions, or for one group rather than another, is considered intolerable at, in, and for others.

19 In either case, actual danger on this score would depend, not on what we ourselves might do in these respects, but on circumstances which might unite America against Jews or Israel as such.

Chapter IV

THE DIFFICULTIES OF THE RELIGIOUS SOLUTION

[1] See Mordecai M. Kaplan, *The Future of the American Jew* (New York, 1948), pp. 79, 211-30. See also the critique of Kaplan's views on this point by Jacob B. Agus, *Guideposts in Modern Judaism* (New York, 1954), p. 408 f. For Agus' own difficulties with the Chosen People concept, see *Ibid.*, pp. 148 ff., 179-87, and for his attempt to solve them, *Ibid.*, pp. 210-27.

[2] For a description of the historical development of the concept of Exile, see the excellent volume by Yitzhak F. Baer, *Galut* (New York, 1947, Volume II in the Schocken Library).

[3] Jacob B. Agus, *op. cit.*, p. 189. An extended account of Dr. Agus' reactions to the idea and fact of Exile, based on this book, would be a fascinating study of the complexities and ambivalences peculiar to an attempt at repressing a fact by sublimating it to an ideal when this is undertaken in full self-consciousness.

[4] *Ibid.*, p. 213.

[5] Mordecai M. Kaplan, *A New Zionism*, published by the Theodor Herzl Foundation (New York, 1955), p. 40.

[6] *Ibid.*, pp. 38-9.

[7] *Ibid.*, quoted from "New Year Message" by Rabbi Philip Bernstein in *Opinion*, September-October, 1954.

[8] "Jews are today without a recognized group status... This lack of group status accounts for the lack of a philosophy and program of Jewish life... The entire mentality of the Jew is deeply, even if unconsciously, affected by his loss of status... The ominous fact about our American Jewish life is that it exists for the most part only by dint of the momentum derived from old-world Jewry... The main reason American Jewry has not developed its own momentum is that it lacks that imponderable but most influential factor: status." (*The Future of the American Jew*, p. 58 f.)

"Modern nations are such not by virtue of blood kinship, whether actual or fictitious, but by virtue of formal contract or decision to act as a body. The qualification of Church membership is no longer required. That change has rendered possible the admission of Jews into the body politic of a modern nation. By availing themselves of that right, Jews have placed themselves in the position of having to redefine their own group status... Though Zionism rendered the Reform renunciation of Jewish nationhood a dead letter, it has at no time taken an official position with regard to the status of world Jewry as a whole. Consequently, if the Jewish emancipation made a riddle of the corporate character of the Jews, the establishment of the State of Israel has transformed that riddle into an enigma." (*A New Zionism*, p. 25).

9 Jacob B. Agus, *op. cit.*, pp. 196-7.

10 *Ibid.*, pp. 304-5. "In accepting the body of Jewish Law, we do not and cannot endorse all the methods whereby the Halachah was brought into being and whereby it developed into its present form. ... The goal of cultivating the spirit of piety and the need of preserving the overall pattern of Judaism should be for us the decisive considerations. It must be remembered that while the practice of Halachah may be accepted as a way of life, its methods of reasoning and deductions cannot be taken up by us if they do not accord with our own convictions."

11 Robert Gordis, *Judaism for the Modern Age* (New York, 1955), pp. 176-7. Dr. Gordis is the writer who seems to see most clearly the implications of dividing Jewry into "nuclear" and "protoplasmic" sections. See his consideration of its difficulties, *ibid.*, pp. 57-68, 180-5.

12 For a technical discussion of the meaning of "myth" and "ideology" see Ben Halpern, "The Dynamic Elements of Culture," *Ethics*, July 1955, pp. 235-49.

13 See R. Travers Herford, *Pharisaism, Its Aim and Method* (New York, 1912), pp. 11-13, 25-33, 36-56, 61-111, and *The Pharisees* (New York, 1924), pp. 29-35, 56-87, 97-103, 107-14; see also George Foot Moore, *Judaism* (Cambridge, 1927), Vol. I, pp. 41-3, 49-55, 57-62, 66-71, 110-21. In later literature on the subject of the rise of "normative" Judaism, emphasis is laid on the extent to which Pharisaism reflects the social and economic conditions of certain social strata. However, the point that is intended to be demonstrated by this evidence is that, *in their effort to make general the observance of the tradition (of which they themselves provided an example of the strictest "orthodoxy"),* the Pharisees developed interpretations which took account of popular necessities. The Sadducees, on the other hand, being satisfied with the observance of rituals by special groups even if the general public could not share it, opposed the tendency to innovate by interpretation. See Louis Ginzberg. "The Significance of the Halachah for Jewish History," in his volume *On Jewish Law and Lore* (Philadelphia, 1955), pp. 77-124; and Louis Finkelstein, *The Pharisees, The Sociological Background of Their Faith* (Philadelphia, 1940), especially vol. I, pp. 121-8. The way in which the idea of monotheism was carried down into popular belief and practice in Biblical times is examined in detail by Yehezkel Kaufmann, *Toldot Haemunah Hayisraelit* (Tel Aviv, 1937). See also Abraham Menes, "Origins and History of the Jewish Religion," in *The Jewish People, Past and Present* (New York, 1946), vol. I, pp. 232-72.

Chapter V

THE CONTEMPORARY SITUATION: A ZIONIST VIEW

1 See Chapter III, pp. 90 ff., above.

2 See Chapter III. pp. 73-6, above.

3 Jacob B. Agus, *op. cit.*, pp. 177-8.

4 There is, on the other hand, a view that, in the suburbs, Jews for the first time scatter their residences among Gentiles and come into closer contact with middle class native Protestants, through town politics, PTA's, and other civic efforts. But, against this, it is contended that, socially, the Jews in the suburbs remain, if anything, even more closely confined to their own company, and this causes the rallying together from which the synagogue has benefited so greatly. See: National Community Relations Advisory Council, *Report of the Plenary Session*, June 16-19, 1955, pp. 7-18.

5 See: Hershel Shanks, "Jewish-Gentile Intermarriage," *Commentary*, October, 1953, pp. 370-5.

A discussion of demographic and other trends towards submergence in Central European Jewry is to be found in Felix A. Theilhaber, *Der Untergang der deutschen Juden* (second edition, Berlin, 1921).

6 Mordecai M. Kaplan, *A New Zionism*.

7 One of the earliest to react to the creation of the State of Israel with the proposal that the Zionist Organization be replaced by a world-wide non-partisan body, friendly to Israel and representing all Jews, was David Petegorsky, a leader of the American and World Jewish Congress. The American Jewish Committee (in spite of the fact that it was forced to establish an international Jewish "Coordinating Council" of its own in order to meet the requirements for representation in UNESCO) has always opposed such world Jewish organizations as the World Jewish Congress, as well as all attempts at a tightly organized national Jewish communal organization, even more vigorously than it opposed the Zionist Organization. For the contemporary American Zionist attitude, see Chapter III, p. 90 ff., above.

8 A clear portent of such potentialities was given recently when, by assuming authority to introduce slight alterations in religious marriage regulations, the Conservative Jews found themselves faced with a threat by the Orthodox to erect a wall of prohibition against intermarriage between two sections of Jewry. On grounds of principle, this fatal step could presumably have been taken any time the Orthodox Jews wanted to for

many decades past (against Reform Jews, for example) but was not, out of a sensible tacit agreement to turn a blind eye to conditions which could have split Jewry, if taken seriously. See: Ben Zion Bokser, "The Ketubah and Conservative Judaism," *Jewish Frontier*, December, 1954, pp. 17-20, and Leo Pfeffer, "Secularizing the Ketubah" *The Jewish Horizon*, June, 1955, pp. 7-8.

9 Both Conservative and Reform groups have expressed their concern at the established monopoly of Orthodoxy as the sole representative of Jewish religion in Israel. Both, too, are making cautious ventures to establish institutions expressing their own spirit in such a way that a direct clash with Orthodoxy may be avoided. See: Ben Zion Bokser, "The Status of Religion in Israel," *Jewish Frontier*, February 1951, pp. 20-4; see also "Opportunities for Reform Judaism in Israel," lead editorial in *Reconstructionist*, June 12, 1953, pp. 3-5; and Herbert Weiner, "The Liberal Religious Impulse in Israel," *Commentary*, July 1955, pp. 38-49, August 1955, pp. 146-54.

10 See above Chapter II, p. 67, and note 15 above.

11 See: Abraham J. Heschel, *Man Is Not Alone* (New York, 1951) and subsequent volumes; and Will Herberg, *Judaism and Modern Man* (New York, 1951).

12 See, for example, the characteristically vague statements by Mordecai Kaplan (*A New Zionism*, pp. 53 ff., 117 ff., 228 ff., 255 ff., 347 ff., 476 ff., 485 ff., and 505 ff.), Jacob B. Agus (*Guideposts in Modern Judaism*, pp. 200 ff., 203-27) and Robert Gordis (*Judaism for the Modern Age*, pp. 77 f., 215-352.)

13 A similar emptiness attaches to attempts of more or less secular theorists to build up a Jewish vocation of alienhood or Exile, detached, however, from the historic course in which these concepts are imbedded and the historic aim toward which they are directed. Exile and alienhood as a *permanent* vocation end in such unconvincing banalities as Waldo Frank's proposed Mission of American Jews to become, as a community, the Chosen Patron of Arts and Letters, the Universal Gadfly and Critic. See reference in Chapter III, note 15, p. 168, above. See also: Elliot E. Cohen, "Jewish Culture in America," *Commentary*, May 1947, pp. 412-20.

14 Mordecai M. Kaplan, *The Future of the American Jew*, pp. 211-30; Robert Gordis, *Judaism for the Modern Age*, pp. 331-46; Jacob B. Agus, *Guideposts in Modern Judaism*, pp. 210-13; Horace Kallen, *Securalism Is the Will of God* (New York, 1954), pp. 78-81; Waldo Frank, *The Jew in Our Day*, pp. 28-30.

15 See Chapter IV, p. 105 ff. above.

16 Mordecai M. Kaplan, *The Future of the American Jew*, pp. 5, 72-81, 142-58, 434-5.

17 Robert Gordis, *op. cit.*, pp. 112-25; Jacob B. Agus, *op. cit.*, pp. 179-202; Horace Kallen, *Judaism at Bay*, pp. 138-69, particularly 152 ff. Waldo Frank, of all this group, is least afraid to accept Exile, though it is not fatality but mission, not the contemporaneous past but the contemporaneous future that he means by it. See: *The Jew in Our Day*, pp. 189-99.

18 See Chapter III, p. 88, above.

[19] See Benjamin Halpern, "Professor Wolfson's *Philo*," in *New Leader*, February 7, 1948.

[20] See Robert Gordis, *op. cit.*, pp. 82-102. In his defence of Diaspora Jewish scholarship, however, Dr. Gordis allows himself to make the opposite and equally fallacious argument that Israeli scholarship must remain essentially "particularistic."

[21] See, *e. g.*, James Parkes, *Judaism and Christianity* (Chicago, 1948) and note the influence of Martin Buber on contemporary Protestant thought.

[22] The idea of completing the solution by emigration with a solution by assimilation of those who do not emigrate has been considered in Chapter III, p. 73 ff., above.

[23] See Chapter III, note 1 above.

Chapter VI

POSTSCRIPT, 1983: RECONSIDERATIONS AND AMPLIFICATION

[1] Charles Herbert Stember and others, *Jews in the Mind of America* (New York and London, 1966).

[2] *Ibid.* pp. 273–301 ("Anti-Semitism in the Perspective of Jewish History").

[3] Of the studies sponsored by the Anti-Defamation League, see especially Charles Y. Glock and Rodney Stark, *Christian Beliefs and Anti-Semitism* (New York and London, 1966) and Gertrude J. Selznick and Stephen Steinberg, *The Tenacity of Prejudice* (New York, Evanston, and London, 1969).

[4] The subject is discussed further in Ben Halpern, *Jews and Blacks* (New York, 1971). See also Jacob Cohen, " 'Jews and Blacks,' A Response to Ben Halpern" in *Jewish Frontier* (September, 1971), pp. 17–24, and my reply, "A Program for American Jews," *Jewish Frontier* (November, 1971), pp. 12–18.

[5] A lucid, instructive account of these matters may now be found in Jonathan Frankel, *Prophecy and Politics* (Cambridge, London, New York, etc., 1981). The Hitler experience has acutely heightened the disposition to take this attitude. It is expressed in sharply divergent ways: *e.g.*, by those who wish to see all Israel's foes in the image of Hitler, like Menahem Begin, and those who, like the late Hannah Arendt, wish to see only such anti-Semites as Hitler (who are equally enemies of all mankind, and must be resisted totally and unconditionally) as foes whom the Jews are entitled to resist actively at all. See the discussion in *Jewish Frontier*, October, 1948, p. 56.

[6] For a systematic presentation of such distinctions, see Ben Halpern, "What is Antisemitism?" *Modern Judaism*, vol. 1 (1981), pp. 255–262.

[7] See Chapter V, p. 130 above.

[8] An outstanding example is Jacob Cohen's review of *Jews and Blacks, loc cit.* Cohen sharply criticizes my failure to take sufficiently seriously the ideological strength of black nationalism (one might add, of Hispanic and American Indian nationalism as well) and use it as a model for American Jewish policy. To what is said on this subject later in this chapter, I may add that I have not been convinced of the permanent commitment of black Americans to a separatist nationalism. The ideological color and strength of their movement is a function of their current grievances and rebellion, and may well decline in the measure of their success in overcoming pressing problems. A better case might be made for Hispanics and Indians, whose nationalism has a local historical base in a sense of national territorial rootage—Chicanos in the Southwest, Puerto Ricans

in their "colonial" island home, and Indians in the areas of their dispossession and their reservations.

⁹ See the discussion in *Judaism*, beginning with Sharon Muller's article "The Zionist Thought of Ben Halpern," Summer, 1978, and continued in the Spring, 1980 and Spring, 1981 issues.

¹⁰ This subject is further developed in my paper "Jewish Nationalism: Self-Determination as a Human Right," in *Essays on Human Rights*, edited by David Sidorsky in collaboration with Sidney Liskofsky and Jerome J. Shestack (Philadelphia, 1979), pp. 309–335.